MAX notes™

William Golding's

Lord of the Flies

Text by
Walter A. Freeman
(BSSE, Old Dominion University)
Department of English
Red Land High School
Lewisberry, Pennsylvania

Illustrations by
Karen Pica

 Research & Education Association

What **MAXnotes**™ *Will Do for You*

This book is intended to help you absorb the essential contents and features of William Golding's *Lord of the Flies* and to help you gain a thorough understanding of the work. The book has been designed to do this more quickly and effectively than any other study guide.

For best results, this **MAXnotes** book should be used as a companion to the actual work, not instead of it. The interaction between the two will greatly benefit you.

To help you in your studies, this book presents the most up-to-date interpretations of every section of the actual work, followed by questions and fully explained answers that will enable you to analyze the material critically. The questions also will help you to test your understanding of the work and will prepare you for discussions and exams.

Meaningful illustrations are included to further enhance your understanding and enjoyment of the literary work. The illustrations are designed to place you into the mood and spirit of the work's settings.

The **MAXnotes** also include summaries, character lists, explanations of plot, and chapter-by-chapter analyses. A biography of the author and discussion of the work's historical context will help you put this literary piece into the proper perspective of what is taking place.

The use of this study guide will save you the hours of preparation time that would ordinarily be required to arrive at a complete grasp of this work of literature. You will be well prepared for classroom discussions, homework, and exams. The guidelines that are included for writing papers and reports on various topics will prepare you for any added work which may be assigned.

The **MAXnotes** will take your grades "to the max."

Dr. Max Fogiel
Program Director

Contents

**Each chapter includes List of Characters,
Summary, Analysis, Study Questions and
Answers, and Suggested Essay Topics.**

Introduction

The Life and Work of William Golding

William Golding was born in Cornwall, England in 1911. As a child and adolescent, Golding, like others in the innocent years before the War, had a basically simple conception of the world. In a generic mode of thinking, during the years before the massive cruelty, devastation, and destruction wrought by World War II, the prevailing concept of man and society included two basic viewpoints: man was essentially good and society was inherently evil. Golding's belief in this concept can be seen in his childhood reading choices which included adventure stories such as *Tarzan of the Apes, Coral Island,* and *Twenty Thousand Leagues Under The Sea.* These stories featured good and pure men in their struggle against the evils of society. He later attended Oxford University where he changed his major from Science to English Literature.

Golding's opinions toward mankind and society changed with the course of the war. He fought during World War II as a member of the Royal Navy. His experience included clashes with enemy naval vessels as well as participation in the Walcheren and D-Day operations. He witnessed firsthand the terrible destructive power of man operating during war, essentially outside the restrictive limits of society. With war as his tutor, he began to view man, instead, as a creature with a very dark and evil side to his nature.

His writings include the novels *Lord of the Flies* (1954), *The Inheritors* (1955), *Pincher Martin* (1956), *Free Fall* (1959), *The Spire* (1964), *Darkness Visible* (1979), *Rites of Passage* (1981), *Close Quarters* (1987), *Fire Down Below* (1989), the play "The Brass

Butterfly" (1958), a book of verse called *Poems* (1934), and two essay collections: *The Hot Gates* (1965) and *A Moving Target* (1982). *Lord of the Flies*, as well as his other works, essentially explores the dark side of what Golding felt was the true nature of man: evil.

He was awarded the Nobel Prize for Literature in 1983 for his body of work, and was knighted in 1988. William Golding died on June 28, 1993.

Historical Background

The critical notes by E.L. Epstein, following the text in the edition of the book used for this study guide, contain an informative interpretation of the story's central image, integral to understanding the allegorical implications of the novel:

> The central symbol itself, the "lord of the flies" [physically represented in the novel by the pig's head Jack's tribe mounts on a sharpened stick, and abstractly represented by the boy's gradual descent into anarchy and violence] . . . is a translation of the Hebrew *Ba'alzevuv* (Beelzebub in Greek). It has been suggested that it was a mistranslation of a mistransliterated word which gave us the pungent and suggestive name for the Devil, a devil whose name suggests that he is devoted to decay, destruction, demoralization, hysteria, and panic and who therefore fits very well in Golding's theme.

In a historical sense, *Lord of the Flies* has been present in literature, literally and figuratively, since Loki, the god of mischief in Norse mythology, and in works as diverse as Dante's "Inferno" and the modern works of Stephen King and other contemporary horror authors. Chaos and destruction have even reigned supreme at times in the modern world. Consider Adolph Hitler and the nightmare reign of the Third Reich, forces that Golding himself fought against, as a prime example of this. But since the embodiment of evil in literature has largely been reduced to an amusing conceit, Golding had to approach his presentation of Beelzebub on a more figurative level. Having witnessed himself the evil that man is capable of, he took a more symbolic approach to presenting what author Anthony Burgess called, "[The] most stinking and depraved of all the devils." In *Lord of the Flies*:

The Devil is not presented in any traditional religious sense; Golding's Beelzebub is the modern equivalent, the anarchic, amoral, driving force that Freudians call the Id, whose only function seems to be to insure the survival of the host in which it is embedded or embodied, which function it performs with tremendous and single-minded tenacity.

On speaking of the same central image in the novel, Stephen Medcalf writes, "The book dares to name the beast, the evil in man's heart, as the beast." Shaped by brute experience, and his dashed conceptions of the good world, Golding's *Lord of the Flies* is, therefore, a study of man's willing (and inevitable) descent into the heart of darkness, fueled by his own fear, and guided by his own inwardly twisted nature.

Considering Golding's own experiences with chaos, fear, death, and destruction on a massive scale during World War II, and his own altered moral philosophy and loss of innocence, it is no surprise that he has chosen to examine their origins in *Lord of the Flies*.

Golding claims to have written *Lord of the Flies* as a response to the novel *Coral Island: A Tale of the Pacific Ocean,* by R.M. Ballantyne. According to *Major 20th Century Writers*:

> These two books share the same basic plot line and even some of the same character names (two of the lead characters are named Ralph and Jack in both books). The similarity, however, ends there. Ballantyne's story, about a trio of boys stranded on an otherwise uninhabited island, shows how, by pluck and resourcefulness, the young castaways survive with their morals strengthened and their wits sharpened. *Lord of the Flies*, on the other hand, is "an allegory on human society today, the novel's primary implication being that what we have come to call civilization is, at best, not more than skin-deep," as James Stern explains in a *New York Times Book Review* article.

Golding's view of civilization and the pure innocence of youth, however, was quite different from Ballantyne's. Having witnessed the grand scale of death and destruction in World War II, Golding described the theme of his own highly allegorical novel *Lord of the Flies* as "an attempt to trace the defects of society back to the defects of human nature." He no longer agreed with Ballantyne's hypothesis that the proper English civilized way of life was good and Christian, and that evil was its antithesis: un-Christian and savage. According to author Anthony Burgess (*A Clockwork Orange*), Golding's characters, unlike Ballantyne's, are inherently evil. Without the restraints of civilization they, "will choose chaos rather than order. The good intentions of the few are overborne by the innate evil of the many. Instead of a boy-scout camp, we get young savages—painted, naked, gorging on pig-flesh, given to torture, murder, human sacrifice to false gods."

Master List of Characters

Jack Merridew—*Tall, bony, "ugly without silliness," red-haired, freckled. He is the leader of the choir who turns into a savage hunter. He rivals Ralph's leadership. His name is from the Hebrew word meaning "one who supplants." His character believes in authoritarian rule through fear, manipulation, and intimidation.*

Piggy—*He is asthmatic and obese. He wears thick eyeglasses or is otherwise mostly blind. He stays near Ralph and constantly but ineffectually tries to maintain order and follow rules. His name implies a relationship between himself, pigs the boys hunt, and slaughter on the island.*

Ralph—*The novel's protagonist. His name comes from the Anglo-Saxon word meaning "counsel." Twelve years old. Fair-haired and athletic in build. Naturally charismatic, he is initially elected chief of the island by popular majority vote and attempts to run the island democratically. He rivals Jack for leadership.*

Roger—*A member of the choir. Slight and furtive, keeps to himself, intense and secretive. Referred to as "the dark boy." His name comes from the German word for "spear." As the story progresses he becomes very sadistic. Allied to Jack.*

Sam and Eric (Samneric)—*Identical twins. "Tow-haired," "bullet-headed," "chunky and vital." They are initially allied to Ralph but Roger tortures them into submission to Jack.*

Simon—*A boy of about nine years of age. His name is Hebrew for "listener." Initially described as pallid, he is quiet, introspective,* *and prone to epileptic seizures. A member of Jack's choir. He has black hair and a low, broad forehead, and is later described as deeply tanned. Allied to Ralph.*

Other boys mentioned briefly are identified as Biguns and Littluns, except for Willard, a character only referred to sketchily. Biguns are the older children, and Littluns the younger.

Bill, Robert, Harold, Walter—*Biguns. Choir members.*

Henry—*Littlun. Distant relative of the birthmarked boy.*

Johnny—*Littlun. Six years old. Sturdy and fair, "naturally belligerent." The first to respond to the conch's call.*

Maurice—*Bigun. A choir member. Broad and grinning. Second in size to Jack.*

Naval officer—*First person from the rescue ship to encounter the boys.*

Parachutist—*Killed in an airfight over the island, his dead body parachutes onto the mountain and is mistaken for "the beast."*

Percival Wemys Madison—*Littlun. Mouse-colored and unattractive. Very small. Cries at the mention of "the beast."*

Phil—*Littlun. Confident. Tells others of his dream of "the beast."*

Small boy with a mulberry-colored birthmark on one side of his face—*Six years old. He is the first to mention "the beast." It is suggested that he perished in the first mishandled signal fire.*

Stanley—*A vaguely described member of Jack's tribe.*

Willard—*Member of Jack's tribe. Beaten for some unknown offense.*

Summary of the Novel

Lord of the Flies is set at a vague point in the future during an atomic war. A planeload of British schoolchildren is shot down and marooned on a deserted island. There are no adults present.

As the story opens, the jungle on the island is severely scarred from the wreckage of the plane. Two boys, the fair-haired, charismatic Ralph, and the fat, asthmatic, thickly bespectacled Piggy, emerge from the jungle.

While they are swimming in a shallow pool inside a lagoon, Ralph discovers a beautiful conch shell. Piggy, slightly smarter, suggests he blow it as a signal for other survivors.

One by one, boys of varying ages from six to 12 appear from the jungle. Among them are several older boys, identical twins Sam and Eric (sometimes referred to as Samneric due to their lack of individual identity), the quiet but strange Roger, thoughtful Simon, and charismatic Jack Merridew, leader of the choir.

While absorbing the view, the boys come upon a wild piglet caught in some creeper vines. Jack takes out a large knife and prepares to kill the pig. He hesitates, and the pig escapes. Jack is upset by what he perceives to be Ralph's condemnation of his hesitation. He silently vows to himself, "Next time there would be no mercy."

Later, Ralph uses the conch to call another meeting. It is decided that whoever holds the conch shell will have the right to speak at the meetings. A small boy with a mulberry-colored birthmark obscuring half of his face receives the conch. He tells the others of a "beastie" that comes in the dark and wants to eat him. Some deny its existence, but Jack vows to hunt it when he and his hunters hunt pig for meat.

Next, the boys decide that they must make a signal fire on the mountain to attract ships to rescue them. They gather wood and use Piggy's glasses to start the fire. In their exuberance and inexperience, they allow the fire to rage out of control and it consumes a large portion of the jungle. The small boy with the mulberry-colored birthmark disappears and is never seen again. It is implied he was killed in the fire.

Jack quickly learns the art of hunting, but still hasn't gotten a pig. While he hunts, Ralph and Simon build poorly constructed shelters on the beach from palm trunks and fronds. Jack returns from his unsuccessful hunt, and he and Ralph clash over the decision to hunt or build the shelters.

Simon discovers a secret place in the jungle. It is a hollow completely obscured by creeper vines. He sits here, away from the others, and contemplates the beauty of the jungle.

As time passes, the boys begin to resemble less and less the civilized British schoolchildren they used to be. Their uniforms deteriorate and their hair grows long and ragged. A marked boundary begins to grow between the younger children (littluns) who play all day, and the older children (biguns) who seem to be growing divided as to their responsibilities.

Ralph, Piggy, Simon, and Sam and Eric see the need for order and civilization, while Jack and his hunters become obsessed with the ideas of finding meat and protecting the littluns from the beast.

Jack introduces his hunters to the notion of camouflaging their features with red and white clay and black charcoal for hunting. This gradual masking of their identities allows them to become more ruthless and effective hunters.

Presently, the smoke from a ship passing the island is discovered, but Jack and the hunters, preoccupied with hunting, have let the signal fire they were tending go out. Jack returns from the hunt, triumphant over killing a pig and slitting its throat himself, only to be rebuffed by Ralph for neglecting the fire.

The boys clash on the matter, but eventually all share in consuming the meat. Ralph calls another meeting to deal with the situation involving the signal fire. Another littlun, Phil, speaks of his dreams of the beast. This again inspires Jack to lobby for the necessity of his hunters. He and Ralph argue again over the importance of the signal fire versus the meat. Jack declares his disgust and he and his hunters leave the meeting.

Ralph considers giving up being chief. Piggy, who fears Jack, tries to convince him not to.

That night, unseen by the castaways, there is a fight between aircraft ten miles in the sky over the island. A dead parachutist lands on the side of the mountain in a sitting position. The wind, catching in the parachute, makes the figure rock back and forth.

The boys, thinking it is the beast, argue over whether or not to approach it.

The boys, led by Ralph with an angry Jack in tow, travel to the mountainside to see the beast. Jack sees the natural bridge to the island's outcropping. He decides that the separate island, joined to the main island by a rock ledge, would make a great fort. It contains many rocks that could be rolled onto the approach path to kill enemies. He and Ralph argue again, and Jack verbally denies any further loyalty to the conch and its power.

The boys' continued expedition to the figure on the mountain is interrupted when the boys flush a boar. Ralph wounds it when it charges him. The boar escapes, but they celebrate the encounter with another primitive blood lust dance in which Robert, pretending to be the pig, is beaten by the hunters who are overly excited by the dance. Ralph's bravery in the face of the boar's charge is forgotten.

As the day wanes, most of the boys have returned to the shelters, but Ralph, Jack, and Roger have pressed on and apprehensively approach the figure. The wind causes it to move and the boys see its decaying face in the darkness. They all flee.

At the next meeting, Jack and Ralph question each other's bravery on the mountain. Jack convinces his hunters to separate themselves from the rest.

Following Piggy's suggestion Ralph, Simon, and Samneric try to maintain a signal fire down off the mountain, away from Jack and his hunters. Jack orders his hunters to kill a pig for a feast, hoping that the roasting meat will draw the others' loyalty away from Ralph. They kill a pig and he orders them to mount its head on a stick as a sacrifice for the beast.

Simon, who had been in his hiding place, contemplates the head of the boar that the hunters had unknowingly impaled near him. He imagines a conversation with the head, and begins to see in it the source of evil on the island. He has an epileptic seizure. He awakens, and the head again reveals itself to him as the symbol of anarchy on the island. Simon has a second seizure.

Simon awakens again and climbs the mountain to view the figure of the dead parachutist that the boys believe is the beast. He discovers that it is harmless, and that the true nature of what the boys should fear, the real beast, is symbolized by the pig's head. He returns to tell the others.

Meanwhile, Jack and his hunters roast the pig, and the others, including Ralph and Piggy, join the feast. Ralph and Jack argue again and most of the boys side with Jack this time. Ralph tries to convince them that they need shelters, but Jack distracts them by commanding another blood lust dance. The boys become so swept up in the dance that Simon, emerging from the forest, is mistaken for the beast. All the boys, marginally including Ralph and Piggy, beat him to death. The tide sweeps his body out to sea.

Back at the shelters, Ralph, Piggy, and Samneric contemplate their roles in Simon's death. That night, Jack and his hunters attack them and steal Piggy's glasses for a fire.

The next day, Ralph, Samneric, and Piggy approach Castle Rock, where Jack's tribe has gathered, to demand the return of Piggy's glasses. Ralph wants to reestablish the power of the conch.

He and Samneric approach the hunters while Piggy and the conch stay on the stone bridge. Jack and Ralph argue again while the hunters take Samneric prisoner. Roger releases a rock they had rigged to guard the bridge. It falls on Piggy, smashes the conch, and plunges Piggy over the edge to his death.

Ralph escapes and the hunters hunt him. He hides near Castle Rock but only manages to learn that Roger has tortured Samneric into joining the hunt. Samneric now fear Roger, the sadist, more than Jack.

Eventually, the hunters corner Ralph in Simon's old hiding place. They flush him from concealment with a fire. Ralph manages to escape to the beach with the hunters right behind.

He comes face to face with a shocked naval officer. A battle cruiser has docked in the lagoon, drawn by the smoke from Jack's fire. The officer is appalled at the savage condition of the children. Ralph assumes responsibility for what appears to be poor leadership. Ralph begins to weep for the three dead children and the castaways' loss of innocence.

Jack emerges onto the beach without his hunting camouflage or weapons. Only Piggy's broken glasses on his belt give any indication of his previous savagery.

One of the littluns cannot remember his own name. The officer, embarrassed by what he mistakenly perceives to be Ralph's undignified relief at rescue, turns away and stares at his warship in the lagoon.

Estimated Reading Time

Lord of the Flies contains 12 chapters ranging in length from nine to 23 pages, with an average length of 15 pages. Each chapter can probably be read in 45 to 60 minutes. A range of 10 to 15 hours should be allowed for reading time of the novel.

Lord of the Flies

Chapter 1: "The Sound of the Shell"

New Characters:

Bill, Robert, Harold, Henry: *Generic members of Jack's choir.*

Jack Merridew: *Leader of the choir. Tall, thin, red-haired, charismatic. He rivals Ralph's leadership qualities.*

Johnny: *The first boy to respond to the conch.*

Maurice: *Member of Jack's choir. Second in height to Jack.*

Piggy: *Fat, thickly bespectacled, intelligent.*

Ralph: *Twelve years old. Tall, athletic, fair-haired. A natural leader. He first meets Piggy, but likes Jack.*

Roger: *A strange, secretive boy. Member of Jack's choir.*

Sam and Eric (Samneric): *Identical twins. Bullet-headed and robust. They do everything together.*

Simon: *A pallid boy, prone to epileptic seizures. Also a member of Jack's choir.*

Summary

The novel is set in an unspecified time in the future during an apocalyptic atomic war. A planeload of British schoolchildren has been shot down and has crash-landed on a deserted island. One of the survivors, Ralph, emerges from the jungle.

Ralph is making his way through the portion of jungle scarred by the wreckage of their crashed plane when he encounters Piggy. They determine that they have crash-landed on an island and some other boys may have made it out of the wreckage. The rest, along with the wreckage, have been dragged out to sea by the tide.

Piggy asks Ralph his name and Ralph tells him. Ralph, however, is not very interested in Piggy's name. As they look around, Piggy rattles on proudly about his asthma and his need for thick glasses. He frequently mentions his Auntie lovingly, but she sounds very overprotective. He has diarrhea from eating the fruit on the island, and must frequently dash into the jungle when he is "taken short."

Ralph works his way down to the beach, inspecting the island. He is initially delighted that it is an island. Piggy follows, and suggests a meeting to learn the names of the other survivors. He tells Ralph his nickname is Piggy and requests Ralph keep it a secret. Ralph cruelly teases him. Piggy is upset at first, but is reluctantly pleased at the attention.

The two boys come upon a small natural lagoon on the beach separated from the island's lagoon by a wall of naturally banked sand. Ralph strips and dives in. Piggy watches Ralph do this, then daintily strips and sits in the water up to his neck. He tells Ralph he cannot swim because his Auntie wouldn't let him on account of his asthma. Ralph, in return, tells Piggy his father, a commander in the Navy, taught him to swim when he was five. He says he is sure his father will rescue them. Piggy tells Ralph that his own father is dead but stops short of talking about his mother's fate. Ralph insists they will be rescued, but Piggy is more pessimistic. He remembers the pilot telling them of the atom bomb killing everyone. Crying, he concludes that, "We may stay here till we die."

They sit around for a bit, discussing the island, when Ralph spies something nestled in the weeds in their lagoon. They fish it out and see it is a conch shell, "deep cream, touched here and there with fading pink. Between the point, worn away into a little hole, and the pink lips of the mouth, lay eighteen inches of shell with a slight spiral twist and covered with a delicate embossed pattern."

Piggy suggests that Ralph blow it to summon the others. Ralph's first attempt is unsuccessful, and he and Piggy laugh at the attempt. Ralph's next attempt is successful, and he trumpets a resounding blast. Soon, Johnny, a small boy about six years old, is the first of many to emerge from the jungle. Ralph continues to blow short blasts and presently others arrive: "some were naked and carrying their clothes; others half-naked, or more or less dressed, in school uniforms, gray, blue, fawn, jacketed or jerseyed. There were badges, mottoes even, stripes of color in stockings and pullovers." The boys gather and sit in a clearing on fallen palm trunks. They naturally gravitate toward Ralph as the instigator of action. Sam and Eric, the twins, come as well. Piggy goes amongst the boys trying to learn names.

Then, in the haze from the sun on the sand, down the beach and into the clearing march the choir "approximately in step in two parallel lines. Each boy wore a square black cap with a silver badge on it. Their bodies, from throat to ankle, were hidden by black cloaks which bore a long silver cross on the left breast and each neck was finished off with a hambone frill." Their leader is Jack Merridew, "tall, thin, and bony; and his hair was red beneath the black cap. His face was crumpled and freckled, and ugly without silliness. Out of this face stared two light blue eyes, frustrated now, and turning, or ready to turn, to anger."

Jack forms his choir into a line. They stand unsteadily in formation under the hot sun until a boy, later identified as Simon, breaks the illusion of order by fainting. Jack orders them to sit and leave the fainting boy alone. He asks Ralph if there are any grownups around and Ralph tells him there are none. Jack then declares that since there are no adults on the island, they must take care of themselves.

Piggy is intimidated by both the uniforms' illusion of authority and Jack Merridew's presence. He rambles on about having a meeting to get names, and Jack tells him he's talking too much. He scorns Piggy's suggestion of taking names, and calls him "Fatty." The others laugh. Then Ralph tells Jack that his real name is "Piggy" and they all laugh harder. Piggy stands, head bowed, isolated and alone.

After the laughter dies, the name-taking continues, and Maurice, Roger (described as a slight, furtive boy whom no one

knew and who kept to himself), Bill, Robert, Harold, Henry, and Simon are identified from Jack's choir. Jack suggests that their attention be turned to getting rescued, and that they should elect him leader because he is the leader of the choir and he can sing a C sharp. Roger, "the dark boy," suggests a vote.

The boys have an election. The choir reluctantly votes for Jack. The others, including a hesitant Piggy, vote for Ralph. The boys appear naturally drawn to Ralph's stillness, attractiveness, and the fact that he possesses the conch that summoned them.

Ralph, the new chief, magnanimously appoints Jack as leader of the choir, and it is suggested they could be the army or the hunters. Jack decides they will be hunters. Then Ralph decides the first thing they need to do is see if it is actually an island they are on. He chooses Jack and Simon to help him explore. Jack displays a "sizable sheath-knife" by jamming it into a tree trunk. When Piggy also volunteers to go, Ralph tries to diplomatically suggest that Piggy would not be any help, but Jack tells him outright, "We don't want you." Piggy protests, but all the boys ignore him.

The boys set out to explore and Piggy tries to follow them. He tells Ralph that he is hurt because Ralph revealed his nickname as Piggy, which he had promised not to tell. Ralph, for the first time, appears to understand the boy's humiliation and pain, but he does not really wish to apologize. He mollifies Piggy by telling him that "Piggy" is better than "Fatty." He tells him to go back and complete the job of getting all the names.

Ralph, Jack, and Simon explore and determine that it is truly an island on which they are stranded. There is a pink coral mountain on it, and a separate island sitting in the lagoon attached to the main island by a natural land bridge. While climbing the pink coral mountain they discover animal tracks that they cannot identify. They continue their exploration and ascend the mountain through thick tangles of creeper vines.

At the top of the granite cliff their further exploration is interrupted by their childish desire to roll several teetering boulders down the mountain. They roll one and it smashes into the jungle below. After admiring the boulder, they continue on and soon attain the mountaintop and survey what they decree as "their" island. It is described as:

. . . roughly boat-shaped: humped near this end with behind them the jumbled descent to the shore. On either side rocks, cliffs, treetops and a steep slope: forward there, the length of the boat, a tamer descent, tree-clad, with hints of pink: then the jungly flat of the island, dense green, but drawn at the end to a pink tail. There, where the island petered out in water, was another island; a rock, almost detached, standing like a fort, facing them across the green with one bold, pink bastion.

They also see a coral reef and the scar in the jungle left by their wreckage. The island appears uninhabited. Simon mentions that he is hungry and the others agree. They decide to return to the others. On their way back, they encounter a piglet trapped in a tangle of creepers. Jack takes out his knife and holds it over the pig, preparing to slaughter it but hesitates "only long enough for them to understand what an enormity the downward stroke would be." The pig escapes, and in the ensuing discussion of how, exactly, to slaughter a pig, Jack mistakenly thinks Ralph is berating him for his hesitation. He slams his knife into a tree again and vows to himself, "Next time there would be no mercy." The three boys return to the others.

Analysis

The first chapter serves to establish the boys' situation on the island, their pecking order, and the introduction of the book's themes.

The boys are essentially stranded on the island and no one from the outside world really knows where they are. They are fairly immature, ranging in age from six to 12, and they possess only a rudimentary grasp of organizational skills. Piggy, the smartest, sees the need for a census but is ineffectual at carrying it out. Jack wishes to be a hunter but does not really know how to hunt or what he will hunt. Ralph is elected leader, but with the voters possessing only a vague understanding of the criteria under which he is elected.

Only Ralph seems remotely suited for his position. He seems to have at least some leadership ability. He understates Jack's election defeat with an appointment to leader of the hunters, and he compensates for his betrayal of Piggy by pointing out to him a worse scenario and appointing him with menial responsibility. He does not appear to know how or why he understands this, but he does. In this manner, Golding highlights Ralph's inherent leadership ability.

The island itself will provide them enough material to survive. There is fruit to eat, trees, leaves, and vines for shelter, and pigs to hunt for food. The coral mountaintop provides a vantage point on the island from which they can look out over the island or the sea. Several references to the small attached island hint at its later importance. The availability of food and the absence of adults is clearly and quickly established so the story can focus on the changes that occur to the boys.

An early indicator of the boys' connection to civilization, rules, and authority is their seemingly natural attraction to the conch. In a realistic sense, they are drawn to it because it is what first summons them in their new and frightening situation. It leads them to their "tribe." But the image of the conch becomes more allegorical as the novel progresses. It is possessed by Ralph, the attractive being who will, through his natural charisma, become their leader. In itself, it is beautiful and graceful and is a natural symbol for beauty and grace; in other words, the polite restraints of civilization. As its role in the boys' meetings grows, it will also come to symbolize the nexus of power around which the novel's central conflict revolves.

The boys quickly fall into the positions for which their personalities suit them. Ralph, charismatic and attractive, is clearly the leader. He is not above using his subordinates for his own advantage. He possesses the conch, which is used to assemble the boys and becomes their focus as a symbol for order, but it was only on Piggy's suggestion that he even knew how to blow it. Ralph does not quite grasp the motivations for what he does, but he does seem to understand the need for his actions. He is a natural leader, a doer, and, unlike Piggy, not a thinker.

Jack's leadership qualities are immediately obvious. He has organized his choir to march in uniform, and he has possession of a knife. Yet, his physical unattractiveness and harsh ways prevent him from being elected. His treatment of the choir (one boy faints

from marching), his contempt of Piggy, and his temper (displayed as he repeatedly slams his knife into tree trunks) strongly indicate his tendency toward savagery. His initial hesitation at killing the pig would make him seem at least a little vulnerable, were it not for his chilling vow to show no mercy the next time.

Piggy is the smartest of the boys. He first tells Ralph to blow the conch to assemble others. He has knowledge of the war that defines their stranded situation and chances for rescue, and he sees the need to organize. Unfortunately, his socially unacceptable physical appearance, his glasses, his asthma, and his weak social skills alienate him from acceptance. He is afraid of Jack and tries to stay close to Ralph for this reason, despite Ralph's callous disregard for his sensitivity to his nickname.

Simon is not yet drawn as an integral character, but the fact that he is chosen by Ralph for the island exploration indicates that he stands out in some manner. His vision of the island seems more poetic than that of the others. During the exploration, when they encounter strange buds on a bush, he declares them candle-buds. The boys' observation of the plant reveal much about their nature. Ralph doesn't see their practical nature because they cannot be lighted, and Jack cuts one open and is disgusted because they cannot be eaten. Simon, however, had named them candle-buds only because of their delicate beauty and their familiar shape.

Roger is mentioned briefly only to establish that he is different somehow, a "dark boy." His personality will chillingly emerge later. The twins, Sam and Eric (later known as Samneric because their identical personalities, looks, and actions blur their individuality) are introduced as robust and friendly boys. The others, at this point, play minor roles and are not fully drawn.

Golding's assertion that the book is an attempt to "trace the defects of society back to the defects of human nature" is the basis for the universal truths he explores. Golding maintains that all that is wrong with humanity lies not in society, but within the beings that create society. With the premise of the novel, he creates a situation in which this can be explored. The schoolchildren are young enough and grow in the directions their individual personalities lead them, undisciplined by social or moral restraints, yet they are also civilized enough to act like proper British schoolchildren if they are so inclined. In this situation, Golding can portray their deterioration pursuant to his thesis. Therefore, the gradual shedding of humanity the boys experience is illustrated through their own defective characters.

The boys, especially Piggy, bring to the island their dim childhood perceptions of society, in particular, the need for organization. Piggy tries to organize the boys by finding out their names in order to keep track of everyone. His failure to do this is due both to his ineffectiveness as a leader, and the boys' general immaturity and unwillingness to cooperate. Ralph perfunctorily sees the need for the names but does not really understand why. Jack does not see its necessity at all. In lessening degrees, with Piggy being the most civilized and Jack being the least, the boys distance from order brings them closer to savagery.

The boys' ability to clearly perceive places and events around them also speaks toward their civilized nature. Loss of this ability is another of Golding's proposed defects. Piggy sees civilization clearly at first. But it is only through his glasses (man-made contrivances) that he can see at all. Ralph understands leadership naturally, but is unable to perceive why. He does not, for instance, know why they should take names, but he knows they should. He does not know why he should not apologize to Piggy for the name incident, but he knows he should placate him. Like a true leader, Ralph naturally and instinctively maintains both a closeness to and distance from his subordinates. Simon views things poetically; he is established as an abstract thinker able to conceptualize and interpret reality. His declaration of the bush's buds as candle-buds illustrates this. Jack sees things in terms of black and white; he should be leader, he should be a hunter, he should find food, he should kill the pig. To him, there is no grey area; his hedonistic needs must be fulfilled. It is the boys' individual perceptions of objects and events that eventually define their positions closer to or farther away from savagery or civility.

Initially, the conch is the central symbol of power on the island. Around it, the boys will loosely form a council in which ideas are communicated democratically. However, as the novel progresses, these forms of communication will break down and reemerge, depending upon the nature of whoever is in power.

For example, at this juncture in the novel, there is no set organization the boys are following. This is shown in Piggy's inability to organize the children for a census. And no one is firmly in power. There is no form of communication at all between an authority figure and the way things are carried out on the island. Later, as the balance of power revolves around the conch, the method in which the leaders communicate their desires to the others will be a telling factor in how they evolve.

Finally, Golding will portray the boys' gradual degeneration into savages as parallel to their loss of identity. In Chapter 1, they are thrust into a situation and a world very different from what they have known all their short lives. This is the first step in distancing them from their identities. Still, at this point, they most resemble their civilized selves. Most still possess their clothes; the choir has full uniforms, robes, badges, and caps (although they quickly discard their robes). They are naturally drawn to Ralph (an authority figure) and to symbols of authority (the conch, with its power to summon). The characters are forced by this new situation to change from their old selves into new roles, but are still, at least, clearly defined within their identities.

Ralph makes an easy lateral move from being the son of a Navy commander to being a leader. Piggy remains an outsider despite of and because of his intelligence. For all his knowledge, he lacks a background in social skills that would allow him to assimilate easily with the others. In addition, he is very pompous with his knowledge, using it to attempt to assert his superiority over others. As a result, they resent and ridicule him. Jack gradually changes from a choir leader into a hunter. These are roles that are changing, but are not very different from what they were back in the society from which they came. Only Simon, slightly different from the others (as can be seen from his fainting spells, which later turn out to be epileptic seizures) remains essentially the same. He is a self-contained thinker, able to perceive things clearly inside his own mind.

As the book progresses, these themes build upon themselves to illustrate the boys' disintegration due to the inherent defects of human nature. Quid pro quo, as Golding intends to show, his island of lost boys is a microcosm for all mankind, and therefore, indicative of humanity's decline as well.

Study Questions

1. Who are the first two characters to appear in the story?

2. What do Ralph and Piggy find in the small lagoon?

3. How does Ralph summon the others?

4. Who is elected chief?

5. For what purpose does Jack Merridew want his choir used?

6. What assignment does Ralph give Piggy instead of allowing him to join the exploration expedition?

7. Who does Ralph select to accompany him on the expedition?

8. What weapon does Jack possess?

9. What does Simon call the strange bushes they find?

10. Why does the piglet trapped in the creeper vines escape?

Answers

1. The first two characters to appear in the story are Ralph and Piggy.

2. Ralph and Piggy find a conch shell.

3. Ralph summons the others by blowing the conch shell.

4. Ralph is elected chief.

5. Jack wants the choir to become hunters.

6. Ralph tells Piggy to get everybody's name.

7. Ralph selects Jack and Simon.

8. Jack has a large sheath-knife.

9. Simon calls the bushes candle-buds.

10. The piglet escapes because Jack hesitates to kill it.

Suggested Essay Topics

1. Examine the characters of Ralph, Jack, or Piggy in terms of what they possess that link them with their past lives, and what their emerging roles on the island are. Is there any indication which of these characters may be advancing more rapidly toward savagery than the others? Support your conclusion.

2. What is the symbolism of the conch? Why does it seem to have so much power? What characteristics does it have in common with what it appears to symbolize?

Chapter 2: "Fire on the Mountain"

New Character:

The boy with the mulberry-colored birthmark—*He is not identi-fied by name because, at the time, Piggy had failed to get the names of all the boys. His birthmark is a strikingly noticeable feature, however. That is why the boys notice he is missing after the fire.*

Summary

Having returned from the mountain with Jack and Simon, Ralph blows the conch and calls another meeting. The boys assemble on the tree trunks around the clearing, which they now refer to as "the platform." Ralph informs them that the expedition has determined they are on an uninhabited island. Jack quickly interjects that, because of this and the presence of pigs, there is now a need for an army for hunting instead of protection. They tell of the piglet's escape and Jack, angry at the memory, slams his knife into a tree again.

Ralph tells them that there are no grownups on the island, and they will have to take care of themselves. To maintain order at the meetings, he decrees that only a person holding the conch shell may speak, similar to a process they knew as "Hands up" at school. Jack becomes excited at the prospect of having lots of rules, but more so because he will be charged with enforcing them.

Piggy takes the conch to speak and Jack looks to Ralph for permission not to allow it. Ralph allows Piggy to speak. Piggy informs the group that no one on the outside has any idea where they are and that they may be here a long time. The others consider this silently.

Ralph quickly intercedes and tries to rationalize that the island will provide them with everything they need, including adventure. The others get caught up in the excitement of this and mention several books of island adventures they have read, *The Coral Island* among them. Jack is excited about the prospect of hunting pigs and asks the others if they have found anything else.

A small group of young boys urges a small boy with a mulberry-colored birthmark to step forward. He tells the others of a big "beastie," a "snake-thing" that he saw in the woods. He tells them it comes in the dark and wants to eat him. The older boys scoff, but the possibility that it could exist remains.

Jack declares he will hunt it and kill it along with pigs. He declares he will hunt the beast. Ralph challenges him by announcing that there is no beast. Fearing that the boys will become distracted by Jack and the beast, he tells them not to forget that they are here to have fun and get rescued. That all islands are charted and sooner or later a ship will come, maybe even his own father's ship. Their fears allayed, the crowd spontaneously cheers and applauds. Piggy openly admires Ralph's ability to charge the crowd positively, while Jack smirks.

Then Ralph suggests building a fire to signal ships. This idea inspires them, and all the boys, including Jack, run off, excited about the opportunity to have fun building a fire. Ralph, holding the conch, and Piggy are left behind. Piggy dismisses them as a bunch of kids, but Ralph runs off to join them. Piggy, acting like a weary parent, picks up the conch and awkwardly follows.

The boys arrive on a platform on the mountain and Jack organizes the choir to the task. Working together the boys enthusiastically pile up dead and rotted wood for the fire. They amass a huge pile and pour on dead leaves for kindling. Piggy arrives too late to help. Against his wishes, Jack takes his glasses to use to light the fire.

The fire is lighted by Ralph as Piggy sits nearby grumbling that he cannot see. The fire excites the boys, but they see it is burning too quickly. They begin a mad scramble through the jungle for more wood, which they continue to dump on the fire. Some of the younger boys stay in the jungle and look for fruit to eat.

The fire grows, then falls in on itself. Ralph declares it unsuccessful because it produced no smoke for the signal. Piggy informs them that they would not be able to maintain a fire that large anyway, and Jack spurns him contemptuously for not even helping. Simon defends Piggy, saying that he let them use his glasses.

Piggy, who has the conch, is upset because people are speaking out of turn. Jack tells him the conch doesn't count on the mountaintop, but Piggy defiantly insists that it does. Maurice suggests green branches for the fire for smoke, and Piggy again complains he is speaking out of turn. Jack tells him to shut up.

Ralph takes the conch and reminds them of the need to constantly maintain the fire, and the need to maintain order and respect for the conch. Jack agrees with Ralph, saying "We've got to have rules and obey them. After all, we're not savages. We're English, and the English are the best at everything. So we've got to do the right things." Jack offers to split the choir into groups to maintain the fire constantly and to act as lookouts. Roger suggests that he has been watching the ocean since they crashed without seeing a ship. He tells them all that they will never get rescued.

Ralph says they will and Piggy takes the conch again. He whines that they don't listen to him and that his suggestions are ignored until someone else says the same thing. They shout him down, but during the melee Piggy notices that a large portion of the jungle on the mountainside has caught fire from the fallout of their big fire. The fire quickly spreads and sends huge columns of smoke over the ocean. Piggy is contemptuous of what he calls their "small fire."

The boys watch and contemplate the power that they were able to unleash. Ralph, made savage by his contemplation of the fire's power, tells Piggy to shut up. Piggy insists that he holds the conch and the right to speak. Ignoring Piggy, the boys begin to giggle at the column of smoke their fire has created. Finally Piggy loses his temper and berates them all for neglecting the building of shelters, for building a bad fire, and for not accounting for the younger children he calls "little 'uns." Ralph tells him that was his job, and Piggy defends himself by blaming the others for lack of cooperation.

Ralph takes the conch, but Piggy continues to complain about his glasses. Then Piggy notices that the boy with the mulberry-colored birthmark seems to be missing. The boys let the fact that the child probably perished in the fire sink in as the "drum-roll" sound of trees exploding in the jungle resounds below them.

Analysis

This short chapter briefly highlights the beginnings of the breakdown in the boys' belief in organization. As the chapter begins, the meeting is progressing smoothly with plans being made and carried out. The anticipation of an adventure like *The Coral Island* excites the boys. However, by the end of the chapter, their well-intentioned plan has resulted in a horrible disaster.

The first meeting the boys have after the Chapter 1 expedition appears to be showing signs of success. The boys have determined a system for organized speaking; whoever holds the conch shall speak. The system seems to work well. At this point, a democratic order is established around the conch. Choices and decisions are shared by all. Together, they determine their situation, they realize they must fend for themselves, and the island looks capable of providing them with what they need.

Slowly, however, cracks begin to appear in the surface. First, a boy introduces them to fear by speaking of the presence of a "beastie" on the island that resembles a snake. Then, Jack's growing obsession with killing pigs seems to be dominating his thoughts and dictating his actions. He even perpetuates the myth of the "beastie," when he knows it doesn't exist, because it will give him an excuse to hunt. Finally, the good plan of the signal fire is derailed by its hasty and sloppy execution.

Once the firewood is gathered, the boys' fragile system of order breaks down rather quickly. Piggy's glasses are taken against his will, the fire becomes uncontrollable, and the power of the conch becomes increasingly ignored. Finally, a brief scene of chaos ensues following Piggy's condemnation of their efforts. Even Piggy, the conch system's most ardent supporter, speaks out of turn. This rapid breakdown of organization is directly parallel to the introduction of the concept of "the beast." Whatever it is the boys begin to fear, it is the fear that begins their disintegration. They do not really believe in the beast, but they do not dismiss its existence either, and the result is the beginning of chaos.

The chapter ends on a far grimmer note than it began. One of the small boys is missing and has probably perished in the fire. The boys slowly realize that the power they possess can have dire consequences. Their actions can result in destruction rather than

salvation. The fire that they so hastily built closely mirrored their uncontrolled passions, and it quickly became destructive. Symbolic of their natures, the fire is power. How it is used, wielded, or controlled is an important symbol for the destruction that occurs later in the novel.

The situation illustrates that once order breaks down, the result is chaos and death. Through their inability to concentrate on carrying out their own plans, the boys quickly learn failure. Despite the fact that they are British and therefore supposed to be "the best at everything," they cannot maintain even the slightest resemblance to *The Coral Island* experiences. Even more powerful than the possibility of salvation is the reality of destruction the boys unleash on the island. In this instance, as well, the fire becomes a symbol of the indiscriminate power of brute force. Unleashed, uncontrolled, its destructive potential is deadly and indifferent, consuming all who get too close.

The explosions from the fire that claim the boy's life cause creeper vines to fly into the air looking like snakes. Ironically, they appear to be like the "snake-thing" the small boy feared would eat him. It would seem the beast he feared was real, only it was not quite what he expected it to be.

Study Questions

1. Where does Ralph get the idea for using the conch to speak?

2. Why is Jack so enthusiastic about the possibility of creating rules?

3. Which boy pessimistically introduces the reality that they may never be rescued?

4. Who first mentions "the beastie"?

5. Who is the last to join the boys on the mountain to make a fire?

6. How do the boys start the fire?

7. How does the fire become uncontrollable?

8. Who defends Piggy from Jack for not helping with the fire?

9. How does Piggy first notice a boy is missing, even though he doesn't know his name?

10. What causes the drum-roll sound the boys hear in the fire?

Answers

1. Ralph's idea for order came from his school back home.

2. Jack is excited at the prospect of enforcing the rules.

3. Roger, the "dark boy," first suggests this pessimistic notion.

4. "The beastie" is first mentioned by the small boy with the mulberry-colored birthmark.

5. Piggy is the last to join the fire makers.

6. The boys start the fire with Piggy's glasses.

7. The fire quickly spreads when sparks from it ignite the surrounding jungle.

8. Simon defends Piggy.

9. Piggy doesn't see the boy with the mulberry-colored birthmark.

10. The drum-roll sound is caused by live trees exploding from the heat of the fire.

Suggested Essay Topics

1. What is the significance of the boys' first attempt at the fire? How does the result foreshadow events to come? What is the result of the fire? Why are the creeper vines significant? How does the fire's result mirror the boy with the mulberry-colored birthmark's fear?

2. What is the meaning of the beast that makes its first appearance in this chapter? Discuss how it is portrayed, and the others' reaction to it. Does this foreshadow its later significance? How does the beast become real to the boys?

Chapter 3: "Huts on the Beach"

Summary

The chapter opens with Jack hunting a pig with a five-foot sharpened stick. He moves stealthily through the jungle on all fours following tell-tale signs left by the animals: cracked twigs, tendrils of creeper vines polished smooth by the bristles of passing pigs, and hoofprints. He sniffs the air for information and examines some fresh droppings. He spots some tracks that lead to a pig-run behind some vines and hears a pig moving in the vines. Jack hurls his weapon, but the spear misses and "the promise of meat" runs maddeningly away.

He returns to the beach where he finds Ralph standing by a marginally successful attempt at building a hut. He asks Ralph for something to drink, and Ralph directs him to a coconut shell filled with water. Jack drinks and comments on how much he needed that. Ralph hardly notices him because his attention is focused on building the hut with Simon. Inside the hut, Simon makes a mistake and the portion they are constructing falls apart. He sheepishly apologizes.

Ralph and Simon are frustrated because several days' worth of hard work has only produced two shaky shelters. Ralph chides Jack for running off hunting and neglecting the building of huts. Jack says his job is hunting. Ralph says he is frustrated because the littluns are not much help. Simon tells him to set them straight, and Ralph complains that they only listen to him for short periods of time, and then run off distracted. Jack claims to be doing his share by working to satisfy the others' desire for meat. Ralph informs him that his hunters follow the same pattern as the littluns and had returned to camp long before Jack did. Jack explains that he was hot on the trail of a pig, and Ralph points out that he was still unsuccessful. They argue harshly over responsibilities for the first time. Eventually the argument dissolves into a discussion of "the beastie." Simon joins them, and Jack reveals that the littluns are dreaming of it. Simon solemnly suggests that the littluns' terrors are severe enough to lend credence to the presence of

"the beastie." Jack claims to feel its presence when he hunts: "You can feel as if you're not hunting, but being hunted, as if something's behind you all the time in the jungle." Ralph is uncertain. He suggests that the best way to deal with the problem is to maintain the fire and get rescued. Jack, tiring of the responsibility of the fire, speaks again of his longing to kill a pig.

Ralph and Jack leave Simon and walk down the beach. Each is absorbed in his own thoughts. Ralph contemplates the fire, and Jack thinks about hunting pigs. Finally Jack speaks again of pigs and Ralph is disgusted. Bad feelings lay unexpressed between them. Ralph complains again of the lack of help with the shelters, and that only Simon is helping him. Jack declares Simon to be strange and Ralph defends him as being the only one who helps and the only one who looks after the littluns.

They return to the shelters and find that Simon has gone. Jack invites Ralph to join him for the hunt later but Ralph's thoughts are still on the shelters. Their unresolved differences lay between them like a wedge. "They looked at each other, baffled, in love and hate. All the warm salt water of the bathing pool and the shouting and splashing and laughing were only just sufficient to bring them together again."

Simon, meanwhile, has ventured off into the jungle alone. He finds a secret place where he can be alone, a small clearing tightly covered all around by creeper vines and a fallen log. "The whole space was walled with dark aromatic bushes, and was a bowl of heat and light. A great tree, fallen across one corner, leaned against the trees that still stood and a rapid climber flaunted red and yellow sprays right to the top." Simon enters this place and drops a screen of leaves behind him and is completely concealed here. From within this new place, Simon's view of the island changes and he now sees the island's poetic, surreal beauty:

> Simon dropped the screen of leaves back into place. The slope of the bars of honey-colored sunlight decreased; they slid up the bushes, passed over the green candle-like buds, moved up toward the canopy, and darkness thickened under the trees. With the fading of the light the riotous colors died

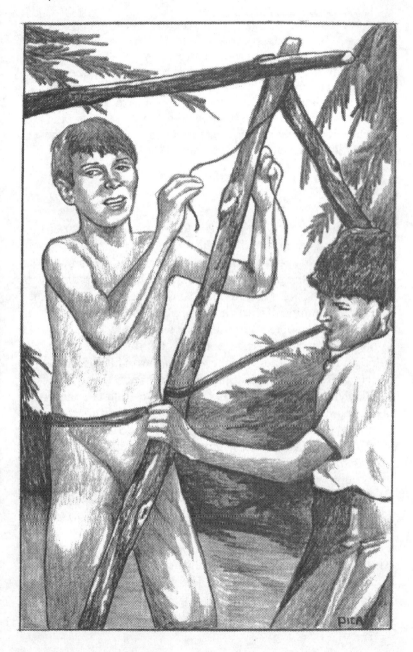

and the heat and urgency cooled away. The candle-buds stirred, their green sepals drew back a little and the white tips of the flowers rose delicately to meet the open air.

Now the sunlight had lifted clear of the open space and withdrawn from the sky. Darkness poured out, submerging the ways between the trees till they were dim and strange as the bottom of the sea. The candle-buds opened their wide white flowers glimmering under the light that pricked down from the first stars. Their scent spilled out into the air and took possession of the island.

Analysis

The themes involving the need for organization and perception are strongly supported in Chapter 3.

Ralph clearly sees the need for shelters on the island, but is frustrated with the lack of participation in building them. Even more frustrating is the fact that Jack's hunters seem to have abandoned their tending of the fire for the pleasures of hunting. Even hunting seems to hold their attentions only briefly.

Jack seems unconcerned as long as he himself can hunt. He no longer requires others to follow rules around him as long as he is occupied. He and Ralph argue over priorities.

Ralph is further frustrated because even the quest for meat that has become Jack's priority is not successful. He appears to be measuring success in terms of what can be accomplished by an organized group, while Jack seems more preoccupied with the hedonistic pleasures of the individual. Neither is successful at this point; Ralph's shelters are poorly made, and Jack has gotten no meat.

That a problem exists at all is only perceived by Ralph. He clearly sees the lack of organization as detrimental. It is only against the backdrop of his perception that the deterioration can be seen at all. Through Jack's eyes, there is no problem beyond his inability to get meat. While Ralph's belief in the need for group cooperation is not enough to make it succeed, Jack's belief in the power of the hunt seems to be moving toward success, as can be seen in the result of his hunt. He has not yet gotten a pig, but he has gotten closer.

Only Simon appears to be acting properly. He quietly goes about the business of helping Ralph build huts, looking after the littluns, and being concerned about their real terror of the imaginary monster not because he wants to, but because it is the right thing to do. He does it because he understands that it simply needs to be done.

Still, he escapes the moral posturings of Jack and Ralph, and enters into the jungle. There, he sees the world in a poetical, almost surreal fashion. Unclouded by civilization, or its residue, he can be enveloped in the truth of their situation. Simon enters a place on the island where, physically and mentally, none of the others can go. Here, he sees the island differently and has an almost communal experience. This shows his ability to be insightful, introspective, and understanding. His vision of the island, and the events that occur, is different. He sees the truth in things simply: the huts need to be built, Ralph needs to take charge, the island is beautiful. It is his ability to perceive clearly that will reveal the true nature of the beast on the island.

Ralph is fast becoming burdened by leadership. He no longer sees the island as a place to have fun away from grownups. Since the small boy's death in the fire, the tone of their existence has changed somberly for him. No longer can his actions be performed lightly, lest they rage out of control again. It is this fear, perhaps, that renders him ineffectual, at the same time making him frustrated by his ineffectiveness.

In addition, Ralph is hampered by his attachment to the fire. This time it is being used as a signal for their potential rescue and salvation. In this fashion, it is being used responsibly and is, therefore, a symbol of responsibility. And it is hard work. Ralph is slowly learning, through his belief in and attempts to maintain the fire, that desire does not necessarily mean accomplishment. In a parallel theme, his power over the others is slipping because he cannot quite control them. The boys, with the exception of Ralph, Piggy, Simon, and Samneric lack the spiritual power that allows them to achieve goals simply because they are necessary. As the bulk of the castaways on the island become more savage, they move away from responsibility and democracy, closer to chaos and the ruling power of fear and intimidation.

Jack's new identity too is emerging, but as it moves farther away from his role as choir leader, and closer to his role as hunter, the reader sees that he can efficiently learn to be a killer. It is this easy propensity for violence that Golding has identified as the basic character defect in humans. It is seen vividly in Jack, and in lesser degrees in the others. But in Jack, it is a conscious attempt at hedonistic satisfaction. He seeks to be a killer because he desires it. As a result, he will gleefully descend into savagery, dragging the others more or less willingly along. The disturbing aspect of this is how easily he can accomplish it, and (as can be seen at the end of the novel) how easily he can revert back to his old self when order returns.

By the end of this chapter, Jack and Ralph seem to be moving in different directions. Ralph struggles to retain what is civilized, as Jack slips further into savagery. It is Golding's point that the latter is easier because it is what humans are attuned to.

Study Questions

1. What sort of weapon is Jack using to hunt pigs?

2. How does Jack know there is a pig in the creepers ahead of him?

3. How are the boys collecting drinking water?

4. Who helps Ralph with the hut building?

5. How many huts have the boys managed to build?

6. What does Jack claim to feel behind him when he hunts?

7. What does Jack suggest will make him a better hunter?

8. Which boy does Jack view as odd?

9. Where does Simon go in the jungle?

10. When do the candle-buds that Simon sees bloom?

Answers

1. Jack uses a five-foot sharpened stick.

2. Jack found the pig's fresh droppings.

3. They collect drinking water in coconut shells.

4. Simon helps Ralph build the huts.

5. Simon and Ralph have built two huts.

6. Jack claims to feel "the beastie" behind him.

7. Jack suggests painting his face for camouflage.

8. Jack thinks Simon is odd.

9. Simon goes to a hidden clearing concealed in the jungle.

10. The candle-buds bloom at night under the stars.

Suggested Essay Topics

1. Trace the path of Jack's success as a hunter and Ralph's growing ineffectiveness as a leader. Compare their emerging viewpoints in their argument together on the beach. What does this say about the two boys and their roles as civilized young men?

2. What divisions are becoming apparent among the boys on the island? Trace the characters and who they are allied to at this point. Discuss these alliances and why they are occurring.

Chapter 4: "Painted Faces and Long Hair"

New Characters:

Henry: *Biggest of the littluns. Distant relative of the boy with the mulberry-colored birthmark. He is teased by Roger.*

Percival Wemys Madison: *One of the smallest of the littluns, a "mouse-colored boy" not very attractive "even to his mother." Plays on the beach with Johnny and Henry. Cries a lot. Thought a little batty by the others.*

Summary

The chapter opens with exposition that establishes the beauty of the island and the lazy rhythm of the castaways' daily lives; they play all day. The midday seems to cause hallucinations in them that Piggy calls "mirages":

> Strange things happened at midday. The glittering sea rose up, moved apart in planes of blatant impossibility; the coral reef and the few stunted palms that clung to the more elevated parts would float up into the sky, would quiver, be plucked apart, run like raindrops on a wire or be repeated as in an odd succession of mirrors. Sometimes land loomed where there was no land and flicked out like a bubble as the children watched.

Percival, who is generally miserable, cannot adjust to the island's rhythm and spends a two-day crying jag in one of the shelters. The others dismiss him as "batty."

The smaller boys are identified as "littluns." They mostly play all day and obey Ralph and the conch both out of a vaguely remembered sense of loyalty to authority, and because of the "amusing content of the assemblies."

Three of the littluns, Henry, Percival, and Johnny are playing on the beach when Roger and Maurice emerge from the forest, having been relieved from their posts of tending the signal fire on the mountain. Roger destroys the sand castles the littluns had built, causing Percival to get sand in his eye and cry. Maurice, from some dimly remembered sense of propriety, hurries away. Roger, now described as having evolved from "unsociable remoteness" to "something forbidding," remains behind.

Johnny throws sand, causing Percival to cry again. Henry wanders off from the others and Roger stealthily follows him down to the water. He watches as Henry becomes absorbed in playing with small creatures in a tidal pool.

Roger begins to throw rocks at him, missing on purpose, not because he doesn't desire to hurt the boy, but because "Roger's arm was conditioned by a civilization that knew nothing of him and was in ruins." Henry notices the stones and is initially disturbed. Then, thinking it a joke, he looks for the joker. Roger hides behind a palm tree and doesn't allow himself to be seen.

Jack interrupts, not noticing Roger's strange pleasure, and leads Roger to a small pool of water at the end of the river where the twins, now referred to as Samneric, and Bill are waiting. He shows them two leaves full of red and white clay. He smears the clay on himself for camouflage as he explains that the pigs, who cannot smell him coming, will now not be able to see him coming. He calls it "dazzle-paint" and the others don't understand. "Like moths on a tree trunk" he explains, trying to compare the situation to something he learned from some vaguely remembered biology lesson. Roger quickly understands.

Jack smears on black with a charcoal stick. He sees his reflection in the water and dislikes it. He washes and starts again, this time planning his make-up. "He made one cheek and one eye-socket white, then he rubbed red over the other half of his face and slashed a black bar of charcoal across from right ear to left jaw." His new reflection excites him and he performs a silly dance that quickly evolves into a "bloodthirsty snarling." His new disguise becomes "a thing of its own, behind which Jack hid, liberated from shame and self-consciousness." He orders the others to follow him hunting, and they are compelled by the mask into compliance.

Meanwhile, Ralph, Simon, Maurice, and Piggy are swimming in the lagoon. Piggy suggests making a sundial using a stick and the others are scornful.

Ralph turned and smiled involuntarily. Piggy was a bore; his fat, his ass-mar [Ralph's word for his asthma] and his matter-of-fact ideas were dull, but there was always a little pleasure to be got out of pulling his leg, even if one did it by accident. Piggy saw the smile and misinterpreted it as friend-liness. There had grown up tacitly among the biguns the opinion that Piggy was an outsider, not only by accent, which did not matter, but by fat, and ass-mar, and specs, and a certain disinclination for manual labor.

Piggy continues to press for a sundial, and Ralph tells him to shut up. Piggy complains that Ralph said he wanted things done to get rescued. Maurice does a belly-flop in the lagoon that distracts them, and Ralph uses the opportunity to ignore Piggy. He casually casts his gaze upon the horizon and spots smoke coming from a ship passing on the horizon. Ralph shouts, "Smoke! Smoke!" but the others cannot see anything. Still, they are confident the ship will see their signal fire. They ask Ralph if the fire is going. Simon and Piggy look toward the mountain, and Simon calls Ralph's name because there is no signal fire. Ralph bolts for the mountain. The others desperately follow.

They reach the fire, which had gone out. The choir members who tend it are nowhere in sight. "A pile of unused fuel lay ready." Ralph is livid. They see below the choir members emerge from the forest waving sticks and chanting. Jack is leading them. They are carrying the gutted carcass of a pig on a stick between them and chanting "*Kill the pig. Cut her throat. Spill her blood.*"

Jack, triumphant, his face smeared with clay, reaches them first. Ralph informs him that the fire is out. Jack does not under-stand Ralph's distress or the significance of the fire being out, and proudly informs Ralph that this time he cut the pig's throat himself. Ralph tells Jack about the ship, but Jack appears uncon-cerned, defending his actions in terms of satisfying the others' need for meat. "The two boys faced each other. There was the brilliant world of hunting, tactics, fierce exhilaration, skill; and there was the world of longing and baffled common-sense."

Then Piggy unwisely admonishes Jack. When some of the hunters, chagrined at the failed opportunity for rescue, agree, Jack punches Piggy in the stomach. Before Ralph can intervene,

Jack smacks Piggy on the head and his glasses fly off and break on the rocks. Simon retrieves them for him. Only one lens is broken, but Piggy is very upset. Jack mocks him and the hunters laugh. Ralph almost laughs too.

Jack grandly apologizes to Ralph for neglecting the fire. His hunters are impressed with their leader's gentlemanly gesture, but Ralph does not accept. He orders the fire lit again. Jack loudly complies, but Ralph's persistent silence both galvanizes his leadership qualities and erects a barrier between him and Jack. When the fire is built, Ralph purposefully goes to Piggy to use his glasses and "Not even Ralph knew how a link between him and Jack had been snapped and fastened elsewhere."

Jack slaughters the pig and they clumsily roast it. Ralph wishes to resist, but cannot. Piggy asks for some meat but Jack says that he cannot have any because he didn't hunt. Piggy points out that Ralph and Simon didn't hunt either. Finally Simon gives him some meat and is ashamed for having started to eat without him. Jack, angry at Simon's empathy, hacks off more meat and orders Simon to eat it. He turns to the others and angrily tells them, "I got you meat," and orders them to eat. The ensuing silence embodies the boys' fear of and respect for Jack.

The situation is awkward until Maurice asks Jack where he found the pig. Roger begins to speak, but Jack must tell the story himself. The others become excited and Jack is careful to let them know he cut its throat himself. Maurice pretends to be the pig and they pretend to beat him. They dance and sing, "*Kill the pig. Cut her throat. Bash her in.*" As the chant dies away, Ralph, envious and resentful, announces he will be calling an assembly with the conch and walks off down the mountain.

Analysis

Chapter 4 establishes Roger's personality and reinforces the themes of organization, perception, and identity. It is here that Roger's personality begins to emerge, unfettered by civilized restraints. As the boys' organizational system breaks down, the possibility of catastrophic consequences again emerges. Piggy's outlook is severely impaired when his glasses are broken, and he slips closer to blindness as Jack edges toward savagery and the

complete loss of his identity. Ralph's leadership, though nobly intended, is again ineffectual.

Roger, initially the "dark boy," is now revealed to have sadistic tendencies. He callously destroys the littluns' carefully constructed sandcastles on the beach. Maurice joins him in this, but feels bad and quickly leaves. Roger, on the other hand, follows Henry to the beach and throws stones near him. This would be simply a game under normal circumstances, but Roger's determination to remain unseen makes his behavior abnormal. He is perversely delighted in baffling Henry and leaving him baffled. He avoids actually hurting the littlun, but he will carry this behavior to frightening extremes later in the novel.

Jack finds he can free himself from civilized constraints and moral responsibility by painting his face and completely obscuring any vestiges of his old self not already changed by nature. By camouflaging his face he becomes the ultimate hunter, even affecting those around him. It is only after he does this that he gets to kill his pig, and it is even noted that he cut its throat himself. It is entirely appropriate that half of his carefully planned face is colored red, the color of blood. Almost savage, Jack has no qualms about attacking Piggy either. He punches the boy, smacks his head, and breaks his glasses. Symbolically, his new identity of violence and uninhibited action result in destroying half of Piggy's ability to see clearly. In other words, Jack's move closer to violence is one step farther away from perceiving civilization for all the boys. He is not yet able to stand up to Ralph, but easily preys on the more vulnerable Piggy. Like Roger, he is testing the boundaries of his new identity as a forerunner for abandoning himself totally. When he revels in the orgiastic feast of the pig, he begins to order the others around and they obey. Jack's sense of authoritarian power is emerging here, and it is effective. While Ralph is unable to get the others to obey him through civilized means, Jack is easily able to exert control through fear and intimidation.

Poor Piggy, Jack's victim, finds his usefulness on the island waning. Even Ralph scoffs at his idea for a sundial. The notion is not particularly useful, but it is Piggy's response to Ralph's directive that they "do something." At this point, not too many children are listening to Ralph. Piggy's one connection to civilization, his ability to see through man-made glasses, is limited when Jack breaks them. His ideas abandoned, his ability to see impaired, he is now forced to view things through one lens. His gradual loss of sight represents their moving away from rational thought. Despite the fact that Ralph will ally himself to Piggy later in the chapter, Piggy and his ideas, like his sight, are slowly becoming more obsolete the longer the boys are stranded.

Ralph's well-intentioned plans go horribly awry when the hunt-ers abandon the signal fire to follow Jack after a pig. As a result, their first chance for rescue is missed. Jack downplays this by focusing on his triumphant hunt, but this only serves to alienate Ralph. Ralph is then put in the unfortunate position of having to criticize the hunters' success. He is frustrated because his plan would have worked had it been carried out. He is losing his power to maintain order on the island. In addition, his belief in the responsibility of the fire produces no tangible result (despite the fact that it was the hunters who failed), whereas Jack quite effec-tively shows his use of fire by roasting the pig and feeding the others with meat.

On a parallel note, the first consciously successful violent act on the island, when Jack slays the pig, coincides with the significant failure of the fire. As the boys eventually gravitate toward violence and savagery, they will move farther away from civilization and responsibility. Perhaps Golding's proposed inher-ent defects of mankind are linked to man's desire for instant gratification, and his inability to reconcile the civilized and primal factions of his nature. Piggy and Ralph are faulty because they do not recognize the power and presence of savagery, while Jack and Roger cannot temper theirs with civility.

Somewhere in between these two differing failures is Simon, who is emerging as a sympathetic figure. He does not scoff at Piggy's sundial proposal along with the others. He retrieves Piggy's broken glasses for him, and he is ashamed to have begun eating the roasted pig when Piggy had none. He even gives Piggy some of his own. He appears to recognize the savagery, and even partakes in its resulting feast, yet he remains able to understand the need for civilization and respect, and can feel sorry for Piggy and ashamed of himself.

Percival represents the basic attitude of the littluns. He is so overwhelmed by circumstances that his normal routines of crying and playing are performed merely by rote. Later, his prominent name (Percival Wemys Madison, so far only referred to as Percival) will become formal evidence of the boys' total loss of civilization. Percival represents the boys' gradual loss of innocence. The longer they remain on the island, the more they forget their ingrained social mores and move toward savagery. In addition, Percival verbally expresses the accurate fear of the beast on the island, the fear of the unknown.

Toward the end of this chapter, the subtle politics of responsibility versus popular opinion will have driven a wedge between Ralph and Jack. Jack will become further allied with his hunters as Ralph, Piggy, and Simon bear the brunt of responsibility. The fire, ineffective in the rescue, will roast the pig very easily and its two functions will also emerge as symbols of the boys' perception. To Ralph it will become the burden of responsibility, and to Jack, the symbol of triumph and power.

Study Questions

1. Which three littluns are playing on the beach as the chapter opens?

2. Who destroys the littluns' sandcastles?

3. What does Roger do to cruelly bother Henry?

4. What substances and colors does Jack use to paint his face?

5. What item does Piggy suggest they build with a stick?

6. What does Ralph spot on the horizon?

7. Why is the signal fire out?

8. What violence does Jack commit toward Piggy?

9. How did the hunters kill the pig?

10. Who gives Piggy meat despite Jack's objection?

Answers

1. Percival, Henry, and Johnny are playing on the beach.

2. Roger and Maurice destroy the sandcastles.

3. Roger throws rocks at Henry and then hides.

4. Jack uses clay and charcoal to paint his face white, red, and black.

5. Piggy suggests they build a sundial.

6. Ralph spots a passing ship.

7. The signal fire is out because the hunters have elected to follow the camouflaged Jack after a pig rather than tend the fire.

8. Jack punches Piggy in the stomach and smacks him in the head, breaking his glasses.

9. Jack cuts the pig's throat.

10. Simon shares his roasted pig with Piggy.

Suggested Essay Topics

1. Examine Simon's actions in this chapter and compare them to Roger's. Both boys are outsiders like Piggy, yet seem to be accepted. Based upon these observations, present an argument for whom they will eventually ally themselves and explain why.

2. What is the significance of the camouflage paint that Jack puts on? How does it affect his personality? Why will it make him a better hunter? In what ways does it hide his personality? In what ways does it reveal his personality? Discuss its symbolic meaning as well as the others' reactions to it.

Chapter 5: "Beast From Water"

New Character:

Phil: *Littlun who speaks of his dream of the beast.*

Summary

Ralph walks down a narrow path, concerned about the up coming meeting. "He found himself understanding the weariso meness of this life, where every path was an improvisation and a considerable part of one's waking life was spent watching one's feet." He is determined that the meeting "must not be fun, but business." He wanders past the bathing pool and contemplates their meeting place (called "the platform"). He notes that one of the essential distractions is a springy log that the children bounce on instead of concentrating on the meeting. He notices no one has taken the time to fix the thing, but cannot quite grasp why. It will be the first assembly they have had so late, and the appearance of the platform is eerily altered by the approaching dusk.

Ralph chastises himself for his inability to think clearly: "Once more that evening Ralph had to adjust his values. Piggy could think. He could go step by step inside that fat head of his, only Piggy was no chief. But Piggy, for all his ludicrous body, had brains. Ralph was a specialist in thought now and could recognize thought in another."

He blows the conch and the others come. Those who were aware of the missed rescue are solemn, affecting those who weren't aware. They fear Ralph's anger. Ralph begins by trying to convince the others that a serious assembly is necessary. He complains that many make suggestions, but few carry them out. He notes the lack of fresh water and the poor conditions of the huts as examples. His attempt to establish a lavatory where the tide can cleanse the mess is interrupted by the littluns laughing at the mention of their loose bowels (caused by eating unripe fruit on the island).

Piggy wishes to speak but Ralph refuses. This gesture reinforces the seriousness of his intentions. He uses this advantage to bring up the fire. Ralph blames the hunters for letting the fire go out, stating that the need for the fire is greater than the need for pig. He begins to talk of additional issues and someone complains that it's too much. He overrides them and impresses them with the importance of controlling the fire as well. He decrees that the fire will only be allowed on the mountaintop. He reminds them that they elected him chief, therefore they need to do what he says. Several of the boys protest and reach for the conch to speak, but Ralph leaps onto the trunk of a tree and again forcefully reminds them that he is chief and they must do what he says.

Jack wishes to speak but Ralph doesn't let him. He says, "Things are breaking up. I don't understand why." He mentions the littluns' fear of the beast and the assembly begins to grow afraid. Ralph finishes by telling them that they must address the unreasonable fear of the beast so they can get on with more important things, like accomplishing tasks, the fire, and being happy. He admits also experiencing some nameless fear, but that it is not of a physical beast.

Jack takes the conch. He berates the littluns for their fear of the beast and calls them cry-babies. He tells them there is no animal. Ralph interrupts, angry that Jack is placing ideas about a physical beast in the littluns' heads. Jack blames Ralph for first personifying the beast. Then, as a hunter, he assures the others that there is no beast on the island. Jack's speech, unlike Ralph's, is greeted with applause.

Piggy takes the conch and attempts to agree with Jack and explain the myth of the beast's existence logically, but the littluns heckle him. Piggy becomes frustrated because the conch is not being honored in his hands. Piggy finally gains the floor and attempts to logically explain why the beast could not possibly exist, and that what they could actually fear is each other. The others do not grasp this and heckle him again. To prove his point, Piggy suggests letting a littlun talk of the beast so they can point out how ridiculous the notion is.

Phil, a littlun, steps forth. He talks of a dream of fighting snake-like things from the jungle and calling to Ralph for help. Then he speaks of something big he saw moving through the jungle. The others listen intently.

Ralph tries to dismiss it for what it is, a nightmare, but Phil insists it is real. Ralph takes the conch and tries to convince Phil that nothing could be moving in the jungle at night because the others are all asleep. Then Simon quietly admits to going to his secret place in the jungle at night. Ralph admonishes him for moving about the jungle at night, but Jack attributes it to loose bowels and the assembly laughs. Ralph feels bad for Simon's humiliation, but takes the conch and tells him not to do it again because it may frighten the littluns.

Simon starts to speak, but resists, deferring because Ralph still has the conch. Ralph asks Piggy to continue, and Piggy summons Percival Wemys Madison to speak of his fears. Percival is terrified of speaking to the assembly. Piggy asks him to say his name, but he cannot. He turns to Ralph who sharply orders Percival to speak. Percival begins to speak, announcing his name and address first as he was taught. He cannot, however, quite remember his telephone number. He begins to cry uncontrollably and other littluns join in.

Maurice intervenes and distracts them from their tears by pretending to fall down. Jack gains control of the conch, grabs Percival, and asks him where the beast lives. Piggy jokes that it must be a clever beast to have remained hidden in the island. Amid the assembly's laughter, Percival whispers to Jack, and Jack tells them he said that the beast comes from the sea. "The last laugh died away. The assembly considered the vast stretches of water, the high sea beyond, unknown indigo of infinite possibility, heard silently the sough and whisper from the reef." Maurice tells them, "Daddy said they haven't found all the animals in the sea yet." And the beast is real to them once again.

They begin to argue and Ralph quiets them by unexpectedly blowing the conch again. This time Simon speaks, even though he is terrified of doing so in front of the assembly. Unfortunately, "Simon became inarticulate in his efforts to express mankind's essential illness." He attempts to explain by asking what they believe is the dirtiest thing of all. His effort results in a crudely anonymous response, a one-syllable word referring to a bowel movement, and his point is not made.

In the ensuing chaos, Jack and Piggy wrestle for control of the conch, and Ralph takes it from them. He notes that the darkness has probably spooked everyone, and someone suggests the beast is a ghost. Many agree and Piggy angrily grabs the conch. "What are we? Humans? Or animals? Or savages? What's grownups going to think? Going off—hunting pigs—letting fires out—and now!" He and Jack again struggle, and Ralph orders Jack to let him speak because he has the conch.

Jack becomes angry, "And you shut up! Who are you anyway? Sitting there telling people what to do. You can't hunt, you can't sing." Ralph reminds him he was chosen as chief. "The rules!" shouts Ralph. "You're breaking the rules!"

"Who cares?" Jack shouts back.

"Because the rules are the only thing we've got!"

But Jack shouts him down. "Bollocks to the rules! We're strong— we hunt! If there's a beast, we'll hunt it down! We'll close in and beat and beat and beat!" He whoops and runs off and most of the assembly follow.

"What's grownups going to say?" Piggy despairingly wonders again. He urges Ralph to tell them how important the fire is. But Ralph knows, and expresses to Piggy, that his advantage is temporarily lost. If he blows the conch, and they do not return, he will lose control permanently.

The hunters and others gather nearby on the beach and chant and dance in a circle, frightening the littluns. Ralph wonders if the beast may exist after all. Piggy argues the logic against this consideration, but Ralph stops him by verbally expressing that he should resign as chief. Piggy becomes afraid of this possibility. He says, "If Jack was chief he'd have all hunting and no fire. We'd be here till we died."

Simon joins them and Ralph despairs about the ineffectiveness of their efforts, calling them "Three blind mice." Piggy asks him what would happen to him if Ralph gives up, and Ralph tells him that nothing will happen. Piggy laments that Jack hates him, but that Ralph is safe because Jack respects Ralph, and perhaps fears him. He finishes by whining about how no one listened when he had the conch.

Simon speaks up and tells Ralph to continue being chief. Piggy tells Simon to shut up and blames him for failing to say that there wasn't a beast. Piggy tells them that he fears Jack and thinks about him all the time. He says that Jack hates Ralph as well because Ralph controls the fire and is chief. Ralph does not quite understand this. Then Piggy expresses his real fear, which is that if Ralph resigned, Jack would become chief. Piggy fears that Jack, as chief, would still be too respectful and afraid to exact revenge upon Ralph, and would hurt him instead.

Simon tells Ralph that Piggy is right and he should continue being chief. Piggy expresses his longing for the presence of an adult to control things. He wishes his Auntie were with him. Ralph wishes for his father, but abandons that line of thinking as useless. The hunters' dance breaks up, and the dancers return to their huts. Piggy again verbally wishes for the intellectual presence of adults, who aren't afraid and who discuss things over tea. Simon and Ralph agree that adults wouldn't have lost control of the fire, or failed to build a ship. "The three boys stood in the darkness, striving unsuccessfully to convey the majesty of adult life." They long for grownups who wouldn't quarrel, break specs, or talk about a beast. Their thoughts are interrupted by Percival Wemys Madison, wailing at the top of his lungs, in the throes of a nightmare, "living through circumstances in which the incantation of his address was powerless to help him."

Analysis

It is during Ralph's poorly run evening assembly that the breakdown of organization is most evident, and the seeds of outright anarchy are planted. Ralph's noble but ineffective leadership skills are highlighted, and Jack is shown to be both manipulative and the cause of the anarchic sentiments on the island.

Ralph is starting to realize that what he wants to accomplish on the island for everyone's good is reasonable. But he realizes he is not a thinker, like Piggy, and cannot control the actions of the others. A belief in organization is not enough. His initial intention to use the assembly as a fulcrum for order is quickly sabotaged by Jack's sly introduction of the possibility of the reality of the beast. In doing so, Jack not only highlights Ralph's inadequacies, but he strengthens his own importance with crowd-pleasing posturing and loud saber-rattling. In addition, Jack's hatred for Piggy leads him to outrightly denounce the conch, the boys' only symbol of order, as useless.

By the end of the meeting, it is Jack who sees what motivates the boys more clearly than Ralph: fear. And it is Jack who will use this to begin his control over the boys. Ralph fails to understand that the boys are quiet and compliant when the meeting begins because they fear his anger. He loses control when the littluns laugh at the mention of diarrhea. He gains it again when he frightens them by talking about the beast. Jack quickly sees this and fosters the notion of a beast, then galvanizes his own abilities by giving them an opportunity to hunt, and therefore control their fear. By the end of the meeting, many follow him. He has united them through fear and intimidation.

Still, Ralph is clearly the generally accepted leader. This is evident when Percival reveals it is Ralph whom he calls for help when the beast appears in his dreams. Jack quickly asserts himself as hunter of the beast, but the littluns' ingrained acceptance of Ralph will take more to overthrow.

Percival and Phil speak of the beast, and the others listen. Percival attempts to fend it off in his own mind by clinging to his full name and address, talismans of a civilization where littluns do not believe a beast exists. But this memory, fading in Percival, is illustrated when he cannot remember the rest of the charm—his telephone number.

The beast becomes real to the boys, if undefined. Jack, the hunter, tries to put it in physical terms, a being that can be hunted and killed. Ralph, the leader, both tries to acknowledge its presence, and yet downplay its physicality for the sake of order and safety. Piggy, the thinker, tries to scientifically prove it is not real, only his theories are wrecked by the diminishing power of the conch to champion reason and logic. Only Simon appears to recognize the true nature of the beast, but he is too inarticulate to express it adequately. His ability to perceive and define the beast does not extend beyond his own thoughts. To Simon, the real source of fear and terror on the island is the people themselves—the boys. It is within them that the beast exists. It is their own fear and lack of spiritual power that will cause the destruction and horror on the island. It is Simon who recognizes Golding's thesis, that mankind's evil nature is inherent in man. Unfortunately, Simon is also acutely aware of his own defect, his inability to communicate his knowledge to the others. This arises from his terror of the true beast, one that is harder to fight than any physical beast: the evil nature of mankind.

As the situation spirals toward the book's eventual violent conclusions, it is the breakdown of communication that allows events to occur. The meetings gradually evolve into chaotic power struggles when the boys, instigated by Jack, continually ignore the order of the conch. It is Simon's inability to communicate his knowledge of the beast that allows it to reign free in the boys' imaginations. It is Piggy's inability to communicate his ideas that allows the contempt of intellectual thought to foster on the island. It is Ralph's inability to fathom the reasoning behind his leadership idea, and communicate their need to the others that allows for the lack of accomplishment on the island to grow. But most importantly, it is Jack's ability to disrupt rational thought, and communicate fear and chaos, that allows him to slowly assume authoritarian control.

By the end, it is Jack who feeds the boys' fears with his promises to kill the beast. By doing so, he makes the beast real. He rides the crest of this sentiment, using it to end the meeting while the attention is focused on him and his hunters, leaving Ralph in a perilous position of losing power altogether. Wise Piggy does not wish this, but more for his own personal safety. Simon, however, recognizes Ralph's leadership as the only link to their civilized past, and therefore the only true protection against the beast. The chapter ends with young Percival wailing from the depths of his nightmare of the beast, now firmly real in the minds of them all:

> A thin wail out of the darkness chilled them and set them grabbing for each other. Then the wail rose, remote and un-earthly, and turned to an inarticulate gibbering. Percival Wemys Madison, of the Vicarage, Harcourt St. Anthony, lying in the long grass, was living through circumstances in which the incantation of his address was powerless to help him.

Study Questions

1. What time of day does Ralph unwisely choose for this assembly?

2. Which matters does Ralph intend to address and solve?

3. Who first speaks of the beast in the jungle?

4. Who first introduces the notion that the beast comes from the sea?

5. Which of the boys is the first to denounce the power of the conch?

6. Who does Ralph chastise for wandering in the jungle at night?

7. Which of the boys suggests that the beast could be from the sea because all the creatures in the sea haven't been found yet?

8. Who recognizes the true nature of the beast on the island, but is unable to express it to others?

9. Who challenges Ralph's leadership by saying, "You can't hunt, you can't sing"?

10. Which two boys desperately try to convince Ralph to remain as chief after Jack breaks up the meeting?

Answers

1. Ralph chooses the early evening when the shadows and diminishing light are changing everything.

2. Ralph intends to solve problems with the fire, shelters, and lavatory habits.

3. The littlun Phil first speaks of the beast in the jungle.

4. The littlun Percival first speaks of the beast from the sea.

5. Jack first denounces the power of the conch.

6. Ralph chastises Simon.

7. Maurice suggests the beast could be an undiscovered creature from the sea.

8. It is Simon who knows but cannot tell.

9. Jack challenges Ralph's leadership based upon his own criteria for leadership.

10. Piggy tries to convince Ralph to remain as chief in order for Ralph to protect him from Jack. Simon tries to convince Ralph to remain as chief because he believes it is the only way to protect themselves against the true beast.

Suggested Essay Topics

1. Trace the references to the beast in the novel thus far. Parallel that with the diminishing sense of order on the island and the boys' gradual embracing of Jack's savagery. What is the true nature of the beast on the island that Simon is unable to verbally define?

2. Discuss how and why Jack disrupts the meeting. What is at the core of the power struggle between he and Ralph? What techniques of anarchy and disruption does Jack apply? What is the result? What does it tell you about the characters of Jack and Ralph?

Chapter 6: "Beast From Air"

New Character:

Parachutist: *Killed in an air fight over the island, his dead body lands on the mountainside and is, from a distance, mistaken for the beast by the boys.*

Summary

When Percival's nightmare ends, Ralph and Simon carry him to a shelter and the boys eventually settle into an uncomfortable sleep. As they sleep, 10 miles above the island, aircraft from the war are engaged in an air fight. A plane explodes, and unbeknownst to the boys, the corpse of a pilot parachutes onto the island. It lands on the side of the mountain and comes to rest in a sitting position, the lines tangle and anchor him to the rock. The wind, catching the parachute, causes the corpse to rock forward and back, "So as the stars moved across the sky, the figure sat on the mountain-top and bowed and sank and bowed again."

The next morning, while the island is still dark, Samneric awake to find the signal fire they were to maintain has gone out again. They relight it from the smoldering coals and in its glow they see the figure on the mountainside. Terrified, they flee back to camp. They wake Ralph and Piggy and tell them they've seen the beast. Ralph has them verbally call the others to assembly. He does not wish to blow the conch for fear of alerting the beast.

In assembly, Samneric receive the conch and paint a frightening picture of the beast they believe they saw, one with eyes, teeth, and claws. They report that it chased them and Eric's face, torn from running through the bushes, is mistaken to have been ripped by the beast. Jack proposes hunting it and Ralph points out that they only have wooden sticks as weapons. Jack asks him if he is afraid and Ralph replies that he is.

Piggy takes the conch and suggests that they leave the beast alone. Ralph almost shouts at him in anger, but fears the beast will hear. He proposes that they go but leave Piggy behind to watch the

littluns. Jack is scornful. Piggy is worried that if the beast returns he will be unable to fight it with his broken lens. Jack chides him for being scared. Piggy defends his right to speak with the conch, and Jack again denounces the power of the conch. "Conch! Conch!" shouted Jack. "We don't need the conch anymore. We know who ought to say things. What good did Simon do speaking, or Bill, or Walter? It's time some people knew they've got to keep quiet and leave deciding things to the rest of us."

Ralph angrily defends the conch. He claims that Jack only wants to hunt and has forsaken the importance of getting rescued. He re-emphasizes the importance of the fire. The mention of rescue swings support to Ralph's side. The boys decide that instead of hunting the beast all over the island, a party will explore the only place on the island where they haven't been, where the beast must therefore dwell: the back of the island where the rocks make a natural bridge to the smaller island. After their exploration they will relight the fire.

After they eat, they set out with Ralph leading the biguns. As planned, Piggy is left behind to guard the littluns. Ralph relinquishes leadership of the hunt to Jack and is relieved to be temporarily free of responsibility. Jack, for his part, makes an enormously theatrical display of hunting.

As they walk, Simon contemplates the existence of the beast. "Simon, walking in front of Ralph, felt a flicker of incredulity—a beast with claws that scratched, that sat on a mountain-top, that left no tracks and yet was not fast enough to catch Samneric. However Simon thought of the beast, there rose before his inward sight the picture of a human at once heroic and sick." Simon, lost in his further thoughts about his inability to express his understanding of the beast to the others, walks into a tree and cuts his head. Ralph, who seemed on the verge of saying something to him, looks away. Both miss an opportunity to speak of the beast.

They reach the bridge and see that it attaches the island to a smaller island of pink coral dotted with huge chunks of rock poised to roll back onto the bridge. Ralph turns to Jack because he is the hunter and must go first, but Jack hesitates. Ralph, realizing the burden of leadership is upon him again, decides he will go on. Simon tells him that he doesn't believe the beast exists, but Ralph doesn't really acknowledge his comment. Ralph moves forward. He does not know what he will do if he sees the beast.

Jack, after having seen Ralph proceed without harm, joins him saying, "Couldn't let you do it on your own." They proceed over the bridge to the island, and Jack instantly recognizes that the island would make an excellent fort. He outlines his plan to use the boulders as defenses, rolling them onto an approaching enemy on the bridge. But Ralph's thoughts again return to the signal fire and Jack is annoyed.

The others, seeing Jack and Ralph unmolested, run across the bridge onto the small island and explore it excitedly. A group rolls one of the large stones into the sea. Ralph is angry because he thinks they should be thinking about the signal fire. The boys argue. Some want to roll more rocks. Others want to return and eat fruit. Some want to stay in the fort. Ralph wants them to achieve their plan, which is to determine the presence of the beast so they can return to the business of maintaining the fire. The boys fall petulantly silent and Jack leads them back off the rock.

Analysis

The beast, previously imagined, has now taken a physical form. Simon still cannot articulate his feelings concerning the true nature of it. The assembly breaks down further, with Jack and Ralph still competing for their differing values. The two boys' perception of the island further highlights their personalities.

The corpse that falls from the sky becomes the physical representation of the beast. As seen by Samneric, the boys' fear has taken on a plausible shape. Ironically, his death is caused by violence, therefore he is truly a metaphor for what they fear. As with most fear, it is exaggerated by those involved. Perhaps to cover up their negligence, or because they are actually afraid, Samneric make the beast very real to the others.

Simon still rationally does not believe in the beast. He knows it cannot exist physically on the island or they would have seen it. Still, to him, there is much to fear on the island, but his thoughts on this subject only conjure up images of man. It is humanity the boys fear. Their own actions have resulted in chaos, savagery, and death. The problem is, he cannot quite grasp how to express this to the others. He and Ralph almost make a connection on the subject, but circumstances interfere and each returns to his own thoughts.

Again, Jack denounces the power of the conch. As he slips further and further toward savagery, he no longer needs rules or symbols to follow. He is becoming increasingly vocal in communicating his scorn of the system. Still, he knows both sides of fear and its power. He continually goads Ralph by teasing him about his fear, yet when it comes time to actually display his ferocity, as in confronting the beast, he hesitates. On the other hand, Ralph, however reluctantly, fulfills his duty. Like the others, he is easily led by fear as well, yet he also conquers his fears in an attempt to do what is right.

Jack and Ralph approach the smaller island for the first time, and their opposing perceptions of it speak toward their differing personalities. Ralph sees it as an obstacle to overcome so they can return to the business of maintaining the fire. Jack sees its military value. Ralph still clings to his position of responsibility and insists they must eliminate the place as the beast's lair before they can continue. The boys that enter the island see its fort potential as well and playfully roll the rocks over the edge. Ralph, growing increasingly adult, has no time for this childish behavior. He must maintain the unpopular mantle of responsibility. Jack seizes upon this in order to strengthen his position, and it is he who leads the boys back off the island.

The contrasts between Jack and Ralph are deepening at this point. Ralph is growing increasingly grownup and urges responsibility. His position is valid, but he still lacks the authority to actually enforce what he believes. On the other hand, Jack is growing increasingly more popular as he goads the kids to follow his childish actions. It is fun to play soldier, hunt, and break the rules. Furthermore, his insistence at disrupting the meetings is personally motivated by his jealousy of Ralph and dislike for Piggy. As seen, particularly in his reluctance to actually face danger, Jack is really not brave. Like a true politician, however, he talks a good game. In dangerously increasing increments, Jack is undermining the frail system of the island and introducing anarchy to the boys. He knows well the motivating and intimidating power of fear, and he uses it to his advantage. The boys have already shown, at the previous meeting, that they are easily lead by fear, and Jack's ability to manipulate them through this will cause the actual emergence of the true beast they should fear: their own evil natures.

Study Questions

1. What falls onto the island during the night?

2. Who is tending the fire when the "beast" is discovered?

3. What makes the "beast" move?

4. What does Ralph tell Jack to do at the meeting when Jack tries to talk out of turn?

5. What do the boys discover when they get to the tail end of the island?

6. Who volunteers to go first and see if the beast is ahead?

7. How does Jack view the island abutment they discover?

8. What do the boys do when they enter the small island?

9. What does Ralph urge them to concentrate on instead?

10. Who leads the boys off the island?

Answers

1. A dead pilot parachutes onto the island at night.

2. Samneric are tending the fire.

3. The "beast" moves when wind catches in its parachute.

4. Ralph tells Jack to sit down.

5. They discover a smaller coral island attached to the larger one by a stone bridge.

6. Ralph volunteers.

7. Jack sees it as a potential fort.

8. The boys roll a large rock into the ocean.

9. Ralph urges them to concentrate on the signal fire.

10. Jack leads them off the island.

Suggested Essay Topics

1. Consider the character of Jack Merridew. How does he appear to be a qualified leader? What are his actual qualifications? Would he be a good leader? Why or why not? Compare him to Ralph. Who is better suited to lead the boys? Generally sum up why Jack's character is introducing anarchy on the island and how.

2. What is the symbolic significance of the parachutist? How and why is it mistaken for the beast? In what ways is it a symbol of the beast?

Chapter 7: "Shadows and Tall Trees"

Summary

Still in pursuit of the beast, Jack is leading the boys along a pig-run, and Ralph is content to follow. They stop to eat some fruit, and Ralph, suddenly aware of the heat and his own griminess, longs for a chance to wash his shirt, cut his hair, wash with soap, and cut his nails. He notices that his nails are bitten down to the quick, but does not remember doing it. Then he observes the others and their similarly disheveled appearances, and notes that they have all accepted these changes as normal.

Ralph wanders down to the beach and contemplates the ocean on the far side of the island. He considers its vastness, and it reminds him of their hopeless situation and their limited chance for rescue. He notes that rescue seems plausible on the other side of the island, because the mirages they experience soften the aspect of the vast ocean surrounding them. Unconsciously, he is tense, gripping a rock, arching his back, mouth strained open.

Simon appears at his elbow. "You'll get back," he says, insightfully knowing what Ralph is thinking from observing his posture. Ralph calls him batty and Simon repeats that he just thinks he'll get back all right. The two boys suddenly smile at each other.

A short time later when the boys are back near the pig-run, Roger calls Jack up to inspect some fresh pig droppings. "Jack bent down to them as though he loved them." He tells Ralph they need meat, even though they are hunting the beast. Ralph agrees as long as they continue in the direction they are going. The boys set off again.

Later, during a pause in the hunt, Ralph leans against a tree and daydreams of an idyllic cottage he and his parents had lived in back home. The daydream is peaceful and vivid. His thoughts are interrupted by a boar charging them from the brush ahead. The boys scatter, even Jack, and Ralph is left in the path of the charging boar. Cooly he flings his spear at it from only five yards away. It hits the animal in the snout and the boar swerves and runs off. Jack returns and searches the undergrowth for it.

The boys pursue the pig, and none notice Ralph's excitement at hitting the pig. They lose the pig's track and in the break Ralph again speaks excitedly of his hitting the pig. This time Maurice bears out his story. For a moment Ralph is caught up in Jack's world. "I hit him all right. The spear stuck in. I wounded him. He sunned himself in their new respect and felt that hunting was good after all."

Jack and Ralph compete briefly for attention from the hunters, and Jack wins it when he shows them a gash on his arm he claims the boar left with its tusks. Ralph tries again to get their attention by showing how he threw his spear. Robert joins him and pretends to be the charging pig. The boys make a ring with Robert in the middle and shout, "Kill him! Kill him!" Soon their play turns rough and they are actually hurting Robert, hitting him too hard with their spears. Jack grabs him by the hair and brandishes his knife. "*'Kill the pig! Cut his throat! Kill the pig! Bash him in!'*" Ralph too was fighting to get near, to get a handful of that brown, vulnerable flesh. The desire to squeeze and hurt was over-mastering."

Jack pretends to kill the pig and they make pig-dying noises. Robert is crying and hurt. They discuss their game. It reminds Ralph of rugby when he got badly hurt. Maurice suggests using a drum, and Roger reminds them they need a real pig. Jack suggests having someone dress up as a pig. Robert ruefully reminds them they need a real pig because they have to kill it. Jack suggests using a littlun and they all laugh.

Later, as darkness advances, they discuss the options of continuing up the mountain or returning to camp. Jack wants to kill the beast. Ralph wants to relight the fire. They decide to go on, and Jack leads them. They come to a stretch of cliff that is unfamiliar to them, even to Jack, and Ralph must make a decision. "By now, Ralph had no self-consciousness in public thinking but would treat the day's decision as though he were playing chess. The only trouble was that he would never be a very good chess player." He tells them they have to return because of the littluns and Piggy, and Jack mocks his concern for Piggy.

Ralph declares that one of them must go back through the jungle alone to inform Piggy of their whereabouts. The boys hesitate at the thought of traveling the jungle alone at night. Simon volunteers and, before Ralph can reply, goes into the jungle alone.

Ralph asks Jack about the pig-run that he had found when exploring this section of the island before. Jack tells him it goes all the way to the mountain, and Ralph decides they will smash through the jungle until they find it. There is tension between he and Jack over the shifting mantle of leadership, and it builds as they discuss the pig-run. Ralph becomes concerned because it is growing dark, and he fears there will not be enough light to hunt for the beast. Jack mocks Ralph's concern as he would mock Piggy, which causes Ralph to ask him, "Why do you hate me?"

Jack does not answer. They stare at one another until Ralph turns angrily away first. He tells the others to follow him and they do. Jack brings up the rear "displaced and brooding."

They find the pig-run and it leads them to the mountain. Ralph and Jack argue yet again, this time over the decision whether to continue, rest for the night, or return to camp. Jack intimates that Ralph is cowardly. Ralph retorts that it was he who went first on Castle Rock. Jack asks the others if they want to join him, and they are silent. He asks Samneric directly, but they tell him that perhaps they ought to return to Piggy.

Jack angrily decides to go and taunts Ralph into joining him. The others remain behind. Inexplicably, Roger joins them. They set off climbing the mountain, and darkness falls. Presently, a gust of wind blows ashes into their eyes, stinging them. They are at the edge of the old burned patch from the earlier raging fire. Ralph is tired and hesitates. Jack taunts him again, and Ralph suddenly outright hates Jack for the first time. Jack continues, and Ralph waits behind with Roger. Roger offers no explanation as to why he decided to join them, or any indication that he wishes conversation, and they sit in silence. The only sound is "impervious Roger" continuously tapping his spear against a rock.

Jack returns and informs them he saw a "thing" on the mountaintop. It made a "plop" sound and bulged. This time Ralph decides to go and look. He notices Jack hesitate for the first time. He proceeds and Jack and Roger follow. They approach and Roger lags behind. They see the creature on the mountaintop, and it is indeed bulging. Ralph stifles a cry. Jack accuses him of being scared. Then the wind blows and the creature looks at them with its "ruin of a face." The three boys flee down the mountain, leaving behind their "three abandoned sticks and the thing that bowed."

Analysis

Chapter 7 sheds more light on several of the boys' personalities, the growing tensions between Jack and Ralph, and the theme
of identity. The most telling scene in the chapter, however, is the
pivotal mock pig-killing scene that succinctly reveals Golding's
hypothesis of the inherent defect in man's character.

Jack is drawn as a more complex figure. He desires to rival
Ralph's leadership, as can be seen during several of the scenes
where he constantly mocks him or challenges his leadership, but
he is not really a fit leader himself. Jack runs from the charging
boar, he fails in his exploration of the island because he had been
previously distracted by the opportunity to explore the pig-run, and
he runs from the beast. He is, however, an excellent manipulator.
To draw attention away from his cowardice and lack of responsibility, he claims to have been wounded by the boar, he constantly
accuses Ralph of cowardice, and he is always careful to appear
brave in front of the others.

Ralph is further portrayed in the dual light of being a leader
and being unable to be a leader. His intentions are always good;
he wishes to protect Piggy, he wishes to relight the fire, he wishes
to return to civilization, but he is always derailed in his intentions.
Sometimes it is Jack who manipulates him away from his responsibility. Other times it is his inability to express the importance of
his decisions.

Nevertheless, his good deeds go unnoticed. The boys do not
really take note of his bravery in the face of the charging boar
because Jack turns the attention on himself. The boys do not agree
with his decision to return to Piggy, until their own fears compel
them in that direction. No one really ever observes that it is Ralph
who truly leads them, and Ralph, unlike Jack, is rarely distracted
from his duties.

One final insight into Ralph's character flaw as a leader is his
own lack of insight. He knows he is not a good strategist (as can be
seen in his own admission to being a poor chess player), but he is
not truly observant either. When Jack hesitates to follow him up
the mountain, Ralph notices the hesitation for the first time. Yet,
in several instances earlier in the novel, Ralph had witnessed other

instances of hesitating on Jack's part. Most tellingly was when Jack hesitated to kill the first pig they encountered. However, he failed or chose not to notice. It is observing this weakness that causes Ralph to actually begin hating Jack and to see him for the first time. Yet, truly, he has disliked Jack for some time now.

Simon proves himself to be insightful and brave. He understands Ralph's longing to return home in the scene by the sea. Ralph has not verbalized this, yet Simon's observation of his character revealed this to him. This goes far toward establishing Simon's ability to understand the abstract, and his ability to see within the character of human nature. Simon also bravely volunteers to travel back to Piggy through the darkened jungle. He is not afraid of the beast, as the others are, because he understands that it is only when he is away from the others that he is truly away from the beast. Nevertheless, the prospect of traveling through any jungle alone in the dark is daunting. Simon does not hesitate.

One progression highlighted in this chapter is the boys' increasing loss of identity. The longer they remain on the island, the farther away from their civilized selves they move. This is shown both in Ralph's observation of their lengthening hair and by their deteriorating clothes. Each contrast with his own daydreams of a more civilized existence. And among the hunters, only Ralph is shown having any desire to return. He longs for a bath, haircut, and manicure.

The pivotal scene in the chapter occurs when the boys pretend to kill the pig and hurt Robert in their enthusiasm. The scene reveals the depths of Jack's growing cruelty when he suggests using a littlun next time. He is always willing to prey on weaker beings. But the truth that is revealed in this encounter is from Ralph.

Ralph does not realize how easily he is seduced by blood lust. Riding the high of his encounter with the pig, he willingly joins the dance and is among those who hurt Robert. He recovers, but does not seem to even realize how close they all came to actually killing the boy. That he slips so easily into this more Jack-like role reveals more about Golding's perception of the defective character of man than all in the novel thus far. If even so good a character as Ralph can be quickly seduced into the desire to hurt and kill, then it is no surprise that the lesser characters follow this path as well. The implication is, of course, that this is a flaw within all mankind. Ralph's inability to reconcile these two conflicting aspects of his character are the root of his flaws, as much as Jack's inability to temper his tendency toward savagery is the root of his.

Study Questions

1. For what does Ralph long when the boys first stop and rest?

2. Of what does Ralph dream when he contemplates the sea?

3. Who correctly interprets Ralph's reverie as a longing to be rescued?

4. What do Jack and the boys do when the boar charges?

5. What does Ralph do when the boar charges?

6. Who plays the pig in the boys' mock pig-killing scene?

7. Which of the boys volunteers to return to Piggy alone in the dark?

8. Which three boys continue to the mountain to encounter the beast?

9. Which part of the beast do the boys see?

10. What do the boys do when they see the beast?

Answers

1. Ralph longs for a bath, haircut, and manicure.

2. Ralph dreams of a cottage where he used to live and of rescue.

3. Simon knows what Ralph is thinking.

4. Jack and the hunters dive for cover when the boar charges.

5. Ralph stands his ground when the boar charges and hits it in the snout with his spear.

6. Robert plays the pig and is hurt.

7. Simon volunteers to return to Piggy.

8. Ralph, Jack, and Roger continue up the mountain.

9. The boys see what they believe to be the beast's face.

10. The boys drop their spears and flee down the mountain.

Suggested Essay Topics

1. The scene in which the boys beat Robert is a crucial development in the story. Examine this situation. What do the boys' actions say about their descent toward savagery? Why is it so surprising that Ralph eagerly takes part in the ritual? Why does he? What do the boys' actions after the beating say about their situation?

2. Consider the character of Simon. How is he different from the others? Why is he unable to express his thoughts? Why does he seem to know what Ralph is thinking? Trace his development as a character thus far, and the emerging role he has in the story.

Chapter 8: "Gift for the Darkness"

Summary

Piggy, upset by the news that the beast exists, stares up at the mountain from the beach. Ralph assures him that it does indeed exist. Piggy questions it again and Jack nastily tells him to go see for himself. Ralph adds that it had teeth and "big black eyes."

Ralph is worried because the beast squats near where they must build the signal fire. "We're beaten," he says. Jack offers his hunters and Ralph calls them "Boys armed with sticks." Jack angrily walks away and calls a meeting by blowing the conch.

He tells the others that he's seen the beast. He tells them that Ralph thinks the hunters are no good and cowards. Jack accuses Ralph of being like Piggy and of being a poor leader. He tells them Ralph is a coward as well, and that he ran from the beast while he and Roger stayed behind and faced it. He tells them Ralph is " . . . not a hunter. He'd never have got us meat. He isn't a prefect and we don't know anything about him. He just gives orders and expects people to obey for nothing." Finally Jack asks them to vote again to see if Ralph should not be chief.

No one moves. He asks again but the boys remain silent. Angry, and with tears of humiliation in his eyes, Jack lays the conch at Ralph's feet. "I'm not going to play any longer. Not with you." He asks those who wish to hunt to join him and then walks off.

Piggy assures him they can get along without Jack anyway, and they no longer need hunters because the presence of the beast will force them to remain close to camp anyway.

Then, to the astonishment of all, Simon takes the conch. Painfully, he suggests they climb the mountain. Piggy scornfully asks him why. Simon says, "What else is there to do?" Piggy takes the conch from Simon and again suggests they are all better off without Jack, then reiterates Ralph's need for the fire to be lit. Ralph reminds him that the beast is on the mountain, and Piggy suggests the obvious that they all have overlooked. They can build the fire right where they are.

"The boys began to babble. Only Piggy could have the intellectual daring to suggest moving the fire from the mountain." The boys are so excited at this prospect, they work to complete the task with frenzied abandon. Even Piggy helps collect wood, and he lights the fire himself as the littluns dance with excitement. Eventually they settle down and drift off, and Ralph speaks again of the need for a census. It is then they notice that few biguns had helped with the fire because most of them had slipped away to be with Jack.

Samneric return with a huge log and as it burns, Ralph sits quietly by himself. Piggy proposes a feast, and he and the twins bring fruit. They eat and notice that Simon is not among them. Ralph wonders if Simon is climbing the mountain and Piggy replies, "He might be. . . . He's cracked."

Meanwhile, Simon has slipped away and heads toward his secret place in the jungle:

> Simon had passed through the area of fruit trees but today the littluns had been too busy with the fire on the beach and they had not pursued him there. He went on among the creepers until he reached the great mat that was woven by the open space and crawled inside. Beyond the screen of leaves the sunlight pelted down and the butterflies danced in the middle of their unending dance. He knelt down and the arrow of the sun fell on him. That other time the air had seemed to vibrate with heat; but now it threatened. Soon the sweat was running from his long coarse hair. He shifted restlessly but there was no avoiding the sun. Presently he was thirsty, and then very thirsty.
>
> He continued to sit.

Elsewhere, on the beach, Jack is taking stock of his followers, mostly his old choir members still wearing the tattered remnants of their choir hats. He declares himself chief and there is no objection. He orders them to forget the beast and they agree. He tells them they will not dream of the beast on this side of the island and they are pleased. He informs them of his plan to draw more biguns away from the conch by killing a pig and having a feast. Then he leads them into the forest where they wound and track a large sow.

They corner the wounded pig, and when she falls they are on her. Roger is particularly cruel, driving in his spear slowly by leaning his weight upon it until the sow screams in agony. Then Jack cuts its throat.

Jack begins to rub the blood on his hands onto Maurice, and then they notice Roger withdraw his spear. They become hysterical because he had pinned the sow by driving the spear through its anus. They reenact the slaughter until they grow tired. They intend to drag the pig back to the beach for their feast. Then Roger notices they do not have the means to start a fire, and Jack assigns Henry, Roger, Bill, Maurice, and himself to put on paint and steal fire from the others.

They decapitate the sow and leave its head impaled on a stick sharpened at both ends as a sacrifice for the beast. "The silence accepted the gift and awed them. The head remained there, dim-eyed, grinning faintly, blood blackening between the teeth. All at once they were running away, as fast as they could, through the forest toward the open beach."

As it turns out, the hunters left the head in the covert where they had trapped the sow, which is Simon's secret place. Simon now sits and contemplates the head as it drips guts and draws flies. "The half-shut eyes were dim with the infinite cynicism of adult life. They assured Simon that everything was a bad business."

Simon replies to his interpretation of the head's mocking expression: "I know that." He is surprised to have spoken aloud. He imagines the head is telling him to "Run away. . . . Go back to the others. It was a joke really—why should you bother? You were just wrong, that's all. Go back, child. . . . " Instead of running, Simon looks around and contemplates the beauty of his surroundings in contrast to "the pile of guts [that] was a black blob of flies that buzzed like a saw." He ignores the flies that, sated from the pig, land on him and drink his sweat while "in front of [him] the Lord of the Flies hung on his stick and grinned." Finally Simon looks the pig in the eye and sees the true beast. He begins to have an epileptic seizure.

Back on the beach, Ralph and Piggy sit alone around their dying fire. Ralph gets more wood, because Samneric are not around. Piggy complains that Samneric should take two turns even though they do everything together. Ralph despairs he is unable to think like an adult, and that "The island was getting worse and worse."

Piggy complains that the others should understand the importance of the fire, but don't. Ralph wonders, "Supposing I got like
the others—not caring. What 'ud become of us?" Piggy tells him
that he does not know, but they will just have to proceed as
grownups would. Ralph continues to philosophically discuss the
fact that he cannot understand why things break. Piggy is pleased
because Ralph is finally accepting him as equal with this conversation. He suggests the problem is Jack and Ralph agrees with him.

Suddenly they are attacked by painted figures from the forest,
Jack's raiding party. The raiders grab burning branches and Ralph
recognizes Jack, "stark naked save for paint and a belt." Jack lifts
his spear and shouts, inviting them to his feast. "He paused and
looked around. He was safe from shame or self-consciousness
behind the mask of his paint. . . . " Behind him thunder booms in
the sky. His seconds announce, "The Chief has spoken," and they
trot away.

Piggy is left clutching the conch. He cannot understand why
Jack did not try to take it. Ralph addresses what has just occurred
to those who have remained with him: the littluns, Bill, Piggy, and
the twins. He tells them that the others may be having fun, but the
fire is still more important, but he cannot quite remember why.
Piggy reminds him it is because they need to be rescued.

Bill proposes going to the feast to complain about the hard
work tending the fire. The twins agree and soon their thoughts of
confronting Jack at his camp are overwhelmed by the thought of
actually eating meat at the feast. Ralph tells them they can get their
own meat, but the others confess to being afraid of going into the
jungle themselves. They sit and think of meat while the thunderstorm builds above them.

The scene shifts to Simon again, still in his secret place with
the Lord of the Flies. He imagines it is taunting him, the voice coming from within himself. He tries to respond out loud, but he has
sat too long and is too thirsty to form words. The beast asks Simon
if he is afraid and he shakes. He laboriously forms audible words,
telling it that it is only a pig's head on a stick. Simon imagines that
the head replies: "Fancy thinking the Beast was something you
could hunt and kill! . . . You knew, didn't you? I'm part of you? Close,
close, close! I'm the reason why it's no go? Why things are what they
are?"

The beast tries to tell him to join the others, have fun, hunt, but Simon, trapped in the approach of another advancing seizure, resists. The beast tells him to forget or else, "we shall do you, see? Jack and Roger and Maurice and Robert and Bill and Piggy and Ralph. Do you see?" Simon imagines falling into the beast's mouth and loses consciousness in the grip of the seizure.

Analysis

True anarchy has arrived on the island. Jack has effectively split the group into two factions, fire makers and fire takers. The fire makers exist on fruit and follow responsibility. The fire takers hunt meat and have fun. Jack is their leader.

The beast has finally made its appearance, and it is represented by the pig's head. It is the Lord of the Flies, in common terms, Beelzebub, or anarchy. The violent rift within the two factions is aptly represented by the pig's head, a grotesque monument to the boys' increasing savagery. The power of Ralph's faction, all of whom are tempted by meat, is weakening. Ralph himself cannot understand why they must keep the fire going or communicate that knowledge. Meanwhile, Jack's influence grows. He organizes the raiding party and steals fire from Ralph. This scenario is not unlike Prometheus stealing fire from the gods and giving it to man, thereby unleashing violence and chaos among the mortals. The fire, in his hands, no longer represents a tool of responsibility, rather it is now a symbol of authority as the conch used to be. In Jack's eyes, the power of the conch no longer exists. Fire is power, and with it he can hunt and roast pig to his heart's content.

Several personalities continue to evolve. Jack truly represents anarchy; he has finally broken from the circle of the conch and declared himself Chief (with a capital C). He uses the conch to call a meeting, but once the group is assembled, he does not honor its authority. Instead, he begins manipulating the boys with intimidation. In the end, when his party raids Ralph's camp, he does not even bother to steal the conch because he has simply created his own society without the need for order. He rules with authoritarian power, without input from the others, and controls them with a combination of fear, orders, and the promise of gratification.

Ralph continues to cling to responsibility, but is increasingly losing his purpose. He cannot even remember why they must keep the fire going; he only knows that they must. Since his participation in the previous hunt's blood dance, he has slowly been seduced by Jack's vision. For reasons not clear even to himself, though, he remains loyal to the conch. He clings to the hope that understanding will come, never realizing that it is his own inability to see this that is the root of his problems.

Piggy too remains with the conch, but even he shows flashes of cruelty. He dismisses Simon as cracked, even though Simon is the only boy on the island that has shown him true kindness. Piggy cannot understand Jack's disdain for the conch, either, but he really only remains loyal because of Ralph's growing friendship and his own fear of Jack. His ability to see with only one eye is indicative of his perception of things as well. He can still see the need for order and civilization on the island, but blinded by the intrusion of violence and anarchy (as represented by Jack hitting him and breaking his glasses), he is more interested in self-preservation than in the spiritual and moral need for order.

Simon, still an outsider, is the only one who begins to understand the nature of the beast. He looks directly into its face and sees the truth. Still, his conversation is imagined and comes from within himself, which is where, of course, the beast is in everyone. His discourse with the beast within himself foreshadows events symbolically. In the end of the chapter he falls into the mouth of the beast as he slips into his seizure, just as the violence that will later consume him and the others emerges from within themselves and devours them. When the beast tells him he is part of him, Simon understands that it is real. And this revelation leads the beast to reveal that because he is a part of them, that is why they have not been able to accomplish anything on the island. Their characters are too flawed.

The true chilling revelation, however, is the full emergence of Roger's character. Previously a strange loner, his personality has emerged as truly sadistic. Even more so than Jack, Roger loves the hunt for the pain he can inflict. He slowly drives his spear into the anus of the sow, torturing it more than killing it. This is the brutal extension of his previous torture of Henry on the beach.

Another indication of the descent toward savagery the boys are experiencing comes through the hiding of their identities with paint. Jack especially is uninhibited when he is made-up; he brazenly steals the fire and dances naked in front of Ralph. His identity is truly transformed and made unrecognizable by the paint.

All the boys know there is now a beast on the island. Only Simon knows where it is.

Study Questions

1. Who calls the assembly to discuss the beast?

2. What lie does Jack tell the others at the assembly?

3. What does Jack do before he leaves the assembly?

4. What is Piggy's radical idea concerning the fire?

5. What feast does Piggy supply for Ralph and the fire builders?

6. How does Roger help in killing the sow?

7. What do the boys do with the pig after they kill it?

8. Who converses with the pig's head about the nature of the beast?

9. What does Jack's raiding party steal?

10. What threat does the beast make to Simon at the end of the chapter?

Answers

1. Jack calls the assembly.

2. Jack tells them he and Roger faced the beast while Ralph fled.

3. Jack quits the assembly.

4. Piggy suggests building the fire near the huts instead of on the mountain.

5. Piggy supplies a feast of fruit.

6. Roger pins the sow by driving his spear through her anus.

7. The boys cut off the pig's head and mount it on a stick.

8. Simon imagines speaking with the pig's head.

9. Jack's raiding party steals burning sticks to make their own fire.

10. The beast tells Simon that all the boys will kill him.

Suggested Essay Topics

1. Trace the boys' gradual descent toward savagery to this point in the novel. What does it say about the nature of the beast? What is the beast? Who are the boys most closely related to it? When has it shown itself already? Where is it? Why don't they see it?

2. Trace the symbolism of Simon's relationship with the Lord of the Flies. Why is the head described as speaking from inside him? Why does he fall into its mouth? Why does he look it in the face? What is the result of understanding the nature of violence? Support your thesis with evidence from the story.

Chapter 9: "A View to a Death"

Summary

Simon wakes from his seizure-induced sleep and makes a decision, "What else is there to do?" There is no reply, even from within. He leaves his secret place. He travels to the mountain where the figure of the dead parachutist rocks in the breeze. Despite his fear, he approaches the figure and sees that, like the pig's head, it too is covered with flies. Simon crawls close to the figure and looks into its face and finally understands what it truly is. "Then the wind blew again and the figure lifted, bowed, and breathed foully at him. Simon knelt on all fours and was sick till his stomach was empty." Then, despite his revulsion, he frees the parachutist's lines from the rock so that it is no longer trapped.

He looks to the beach and sees the boys far away, and he sees too that the fire, which they moved to be away from the beast, is out. He decides, "The beast was harmless and horrible; and the news must reach the others as soon as possible." He starts toward them down the mountain.

Back at the lagoon, Piggy and Ralph are bathing idly in the pool. Ralph squirts some water at Piggy. They muse about the whereabouts of the others. Piggy says they have gone to join Jack's party, "Just for some meat." Ralph says he doesn't care. Piggy suggests joining them, and Ralph stares at him until he adds, "I mean—to make sure nothing happens." Ralph squirts some more water at his friend.

Ralph and Piggy approach Jack's lot and hear the sounds of the party. They see the pig roasting over a fire and most of the boys lying around drinking from coconut shells. The others see them and all are silent. Ralph and Piggy approach. One of the boys tending the pig tears off a chunk of hot meat and burns Piggy with it as he runs past. Piggy yells and dances about and they all laugh at him. "Piggy once more was the center of social derision so that everyone felt cheerful and normal."

Jack orders them some meat, and orders the others to eat all they want. He demands drink, and Henry obediently brings him

some. He tells them to sit and all but Ralph and Piggy obey. He asks who will join his tribe, and Ralph tells him he is still chief.

They proceed to argue about possession of the conch and its boundaries of authority on the island. Several agree to join Jack and Ralph threatens to blow the conch for a meeting. Jack tells him that no one will listen. Piggy tries to get Ralph to leave.

Meanwhile, a huge thunderstorm is building above them. Ralph asks them what the hunters will do in the rain without shelters. Then it begins to rain, and several littluns start panicking.

Jack orders everyone to do their ritual dance. They form a circle and Roger pretends to be the pig in the middle. They chant, "*Kill the beast! Cut his throat! Spill his blood!*" Piggy and Ralph, intimidated by the coming storm, join the circle. Lightning and thunder burst above them. "Now out of the terror rose another desire, thick, urgent, blind."

At this moment, Simon emerges from the forest screaming about a dead man on a hill. He wanders into the center of the circle. The boys mistake him for the beast, fall on him, and beat him as he screams something about a body on the hill. Simon staggers to the edge of the rocks and falls over onto the beach. The boys descend upon him again, screaming and biting, and beat him to death in the sand. One by one they break up and stagger away. "Only the beast lay still, a few yards from the sea. Even in the rain they could see how small a beast it was; and already its blood was staining the sand."

High up on the mountain, the wind catches the parachute of the dead man and carries it toward the boys as if it were awkwardly walking over the tops of the trees. The boys scatter in fear at the sight of this horrid apparition in the wind, lightning, and rain. The body is carried out to sea by the storm.

Presently, the gale wanes and the tide comes in. With it are strange creatures that glow in the dark. The water and the glowing creatures surround Simon's body and cleanse it of blood.

Analysis

Several of the novel's themes are reinforced in this chapter, but it is Golding's evocative description of Simon's death and burial at sea that form the chapter's compelling core.

The boys continue to move away from order and responsibility. They have joined Jack to satisfy their inherent craving for meat, and have forsaken the wisdom of shelters and responsibility. This hedonistic lifestyle is so powerful that even Ralph and Piggy join in the Bacchanalian debauch. Golding's description of the feast places it in terms of a Roman orgiastic feast, itself a symbol of mankind's descent into savagery through its own base desires. As the Roman empire became corrupt, with the focus more upon self-gratification, so do the boys descend. They lay about, gnawing meat down to the bone while, "Jack, painted and garlanded, sat there like an idol. There were piles of meat on green leaves near him, and fruit, and coconut shells full of drink."

Piggy and Ralph experience slight losses of their identities. Around the bathing pool they reveal this slide. Ralph no longer cares who joins Jack. Even Piggy suggests joining him for some meat. These utterances illustrate their own inherent weaknesses and make it plausible when they join the murderous circle later.

The conch is abandoned by Jack for good. He has completely broken from its power and has installed himself as absolute leader, replacing the democratic process with his authoritarian absolute rule. Like a dictator he orders those who follow him about, and they obey. He openly refuses the conch's power by declaring none will listen if Ralph blows it. It is telling that Ralph has not even brought it to this feast.

But it is around Simon that this chapter truly focuses its message. His awakening in the clearing and subsequent discovery of the true nature of the beast are described in the beautifully poetic prose Golding reserves for Simon's character alone. This subtle choice of description implies a relationship between violence and beauty in regard to man. Spiritually, only Simon truly understands the beast, but to do so he must look it directly in the face and confront it. Only by opening himself up to truth and beauty, can he achieve the vision needed to see into the core of humanity and spot the beast. The discovery of the true nature of the beast is that, at its center, it is man. In order for there to be chaos and decay, there must first be beauty. In Simon's idyllic retreat, the corpse of the pig has drawn flies that devour it and replace the butterflies that swarmed there. Likewise, the corpse of the man, nature's beautiful creation, is, like the pig's head, rotting and covered with flies. The focus of these flies, who worship at the temple of their lord, is death by violence, the ultimate destruction of beauty.

On a symbolic level, it is the forces of nature that brings the beast to the boys spiritually and symbolically. Simon had to travel to the mountain to view the beast and understand it. Since he was inherently peaceful, his spiritual attempts to understand his own violent nature forced him to seek out the face of the beast to confront it. On the other hand, the boys, who are inherently violent, succumb to their natures and kill Simon, and the beast has truly arrived. This happens both spiritually when they commit the violence, and symbolically when the wind carries the corpse of the airman to them over the trees.

Simon's burial at sea by the magical glowing creatures is described in the same implications of duality. But the content of the chapter's final paragraph, Golding's description of the cleansing and removal of the corpse, suggests there is a relationship between man's violent nature and the natural order of the world. Simon is lifted and carried away by forces that derive their power from the core of the earth in its manipulation of the tides. This suggested relationship is central to Golding's theme that the great violent natural tendencies of humans are due to a flaw inherent in man's character, a flaw planted naturally, and from which there is no civilized escape.

Study Questions

1. In Simon's secret place, which source of food do the flies prefer?

2. Where does Simon decide to go?

3. What does Simon do to the figure on the mountainside?

4. Who suggests Ralph and Piggy should go to the party?

5. How is it that Ralph and Piggy's awkward presence at the party is accepted?

6. What does Jack declare about the conch to Ralph?

7. What is the weather like toward the end of the party?

8. What chant do the boys sing as they dance?

9. Who emerges from the jungle with the secret of the beast?

10. What scares the boys and sends them scattering?

Answers

1. The flies prefer the pig's blood to the blood from Simon's nose.

2. Simon decides to travel to the mountain and look into the face of the beast.

3. Simon frees the parachutist's lines from the rock.

4. Piggy suggests that he and Ralph join Jack's party.

5. The boys all laugh at Piggy and that breaks the tension.

6. Jack declares he will no longer obey the conch.

7. The weather becomes threatening: rain, thunder, and lightning.

8. The boys chant, "*Kill the beast! Cut his throat! Spill his blood!*"

9. Simon emerges from the jungle and is killed before he can reveal the secret of the beast.

10. The boys scatter at the sight of the dead parachutist "walking" along the treetops as he is carried by the wind.

Suggested Essay Topics

1. Why does Simon travel to the mountaintop? What does he do there? What does he discover there? What is the symbolic meaning of his journey and discovery?

2. What is the meaning behind Simon's death? How and why is he killed? What is he doing when he is killed? Why do Ralph and Piggy have a part in his death? What part do they play?

Chapter 10: "The Shell and the Glasses"

New Characters:

Willard: *A member of Jack's tribe, beaten in punishment for an un-named offense.*

Stanley: *Tribal member, asks if they really killed Simon.*

Summary

Piggy carefully watches Ralph approach. Somehow, Ralph still maintains his leadership charisma, despite what happened to Simon. He is limping, bruised, and has dead leaves in his hair. Together, they determine that only Ralph, Piggy, Samneric, and some littluns remain loyal to the conch. Ralph and Piggy sit on the platform facing the shell.

Ralph begins to talk about Simon and what happened. He says it was murder. Piggy insists that it is no good to talk about it like that. He says it was only because they were scared. "I wasn't scared," said Ralph slowly, "I was—I don't know what I was." Piggy suggests, desperately, that Simon may still be alive and that he was only pretending. He suggests that maybe it was an accident.

Ralph says, "I'm frightened. Of us. I want to go home. Oh God, I want to go home." Piggy insists again it was an accident. Piggy says they should not tell Samneric that they were at the dance, and they then rationalize that they were only on the outskirts of the dance and not really participants after all. Piggy says the four of them can live by themselves and keep the fire going.

Samneric emerge from the jungle with wood. The moment is awkward. Soon they all begin making clumsy excuses as to why they were not at the dance's conclusion. They all insist they left early, despite the fact that each of them bears physical wounds from the frenzied encounter.

On the other side of the island, Roger approaches the small outcropping attached to the main island that the boys call Castle Rock. He is not surprised to be challenged by a sentry who identifies him and allows him to pass. Roger tells him he could have passed easily if he wanted to, and the sentry shows him their defenses. A log has been placed as a lever under a huge rock, ready to topple it down onto the pathway if necessary. Roger admires Jack's leadership. The sentry tells him they are beating a boy named Willard that afternoon for some unknown reason. Roger considers this briefly, "assimilating the possibilities of irresponsible authority." Then he joins the others.

Jack is holding council, naked to the waist, his face painted in white and red. Willard lies sniveling in the background, having been beaten. Jack promises his tribe they will hunt again tomorrow. He assures them the gate is securely guarded against the others sneaking in. When a tribe member asks why they would even try, Jack's reply is "vague but earnest." He says they will try to spoil things. He also says the beast might try again, after having already attempted to come in disguise. The others shudder in agreement.

Stanley wants to ask if they really killed Simon, but he cannot quite finish the words. Jack insists they did not, but each tribe member reacts internally to the truth. Jack orders them to sacrifice the head of all kills to the beast. Stanley agrees it was the beast. Jack says it is best to keep on the good side of it. He promises a feast for tomorrow, and Bill asks what they will use to light the fire. Jack secretly blushes behind his paint, but then commands that they will steal fire from the others. Roger and Maurice volunteer to accompany Jack on the mission.

Back on the beach, Ralph is using Piggy's glasses to light a fire. They verbally long to be rescued. When someone determines they need more wood, Piggy claims he cannot carry any because of his asthma. The other boys fetch some until Eric complains he is too tired to carry any more wood. "What's the good?"

Ralph encourages him not to think that way but cannot remember why. Piggy reminds him that it is for the rescue. They discuss the difficulties of tending the fire always, and Ralph allows them to let it go for the night. No one wants to look for wood in the dark anyway, so they return to the shelters and try to sleep.

Ralph thinks about being rescued and returning home. He inadvertently makes a noise that frightens Piggy, who asks him not to do that. In another corner of the shelter, Samneric are wrestling each other while locked in the throes of a nightmare. Piggy and Ralph shout and they calm down.

Piggy tells Ralph that they really need to be rescued or they will go crazy. Ralph sarcastically suggests he mail a letter to his aunt. Piggy replies solemnly, "I don't know where she is now. And I haven't got an envelope and a stamp. An' there isn't a mailbox. Or a postman." Ralph laughs uncontrollably and Piggy cannot understand why.

Then they hear something moving outside and, fearing the beast, become quiet. "Desperately, Ralph prayed that the beast would prefer littluns." From the jungle, voices call for Piggy, and Ralph tells him to remain silent. Piggy has an asthma attack at the same time Jack's tribe members assault them.

There is general confusion. Ralph is punched in the nose but gets the better of his opponent. He pummels the face below him until his opponent kicks him between the legs and he rolls off. The shelter collapses and the attackers disappear back into the jungle.

They drag Piggy clear and assess the damage. Unbeknownst to Ralph and Eric, their stories reveal they were beating each other. Ralph was pummeling Eric's face, and Eric kicked Ralph between the legs. The boys never realize the truth of this. Piggy says he *thought* they were going for the conch, and Ralph checks and tells him it is still there. But Piggy says, "I know. They didn't come for the conch. They came for something else. Ralph—what am I going to do?"

Down the beach, the attackers run along and dance triumphantly. Jack leads their victory, his chiefdom now secure. He stabs the air with his spear while Piggy's glasses dangle from his left hand.

Analysis

The last vestiges of civilization disappear in this chapter. Jack's tribe is firmly in place, and Jack is accepted as its leader. As a leader, he is better than Ralph at achieving his goals; it is only that his goals are destructive. Unlike Ralph, Jack's leadership involves intimidation and fear. He orders his tribe around and beats those who don't obey.

Where Ralph is unable to quell his followers' misery over Simon's death, Jack is able to assuage his followers' doubts. Ralph fails with the truth and flimsy rationalization, while Jack assertively covers the truth with empty rhetoric.

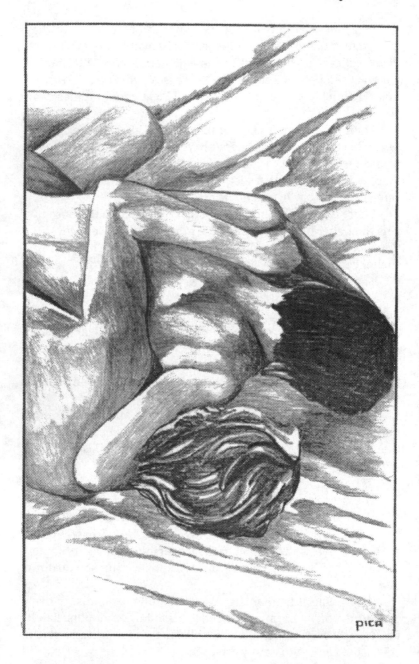

Ralph is unable to organize the fire and cannot even remember why it is important. Jack sets a clear goal for his tribe, and they carry it out. The stealing of Piggy's glasses represents not only the triumph of violence and chaos, but the destruction of civilization and vision. Piggy, the one true believer in the sanctity of the conch and order, is now blind and helpless.

Further indications of the ineffectiveness of civilization in the face of chaos are the feeble attempts of Ralph and Eric to fend off their attackers. They blindly fight one another and succeed only in becoming their own worst enemies. Not recognizing the primitive sides of their own nature, they struggle with themselves and are ultimately self-destructive.

Jack leads his tribe behind his mask of paint, which camouflages his own shortcomings. His followers cannot see his inability to take the fire into account as he blushes at forgetting they don't possess it. They can, however, see his instant decision to steal the fire and they follow blindly.

Roger again emerges as a figure whose frightening personality could rival Jack's. When the sentry tells him Jack is beating a follower, Roger muses on the *possibilities* of irresponsible authority. In such an atmosphere, where there are no legal or moral restraints, he is free to act as he pleases and satisfy his sadistic tendencies. Whereas Jack is acting in his capacity to submit his own brand of anarchic rule, Roger sees it as an opportunity to indulge his dark desires. He is more deliberate in his approach to chaos than Jack. Unlike Jack, who sees it as necessity, Roger views it as opportunity. He is the worst result of the breakdown of authority.

The conch has become meaningless. Its usefulness has been so limited, it is no longer even a target for Jack's usurpation of power. Fire has taken its place and represents the true mantle of power on the island. Fire, which could have been used for good, is now captured and subjugated to serving a bestial master and his bestial desires. Fire is power, and Jack now wields it.

With Simon dead there is no longer any chance of understanding the terrible nature of humanity on the island. Ralph comes close to Simon's insight when he admits to being frightened of himself and the others, but he cannot understand why. He does not see the beast inside his own nature, and therefore cannot recognize what he is fighting against. This is related to his inability to remember why they must maintain the fire for rescue. The beast is loose. The Lord of the Flies has unlimited dominion over the boys.

Study Questions

1. Who is left among the boys that remain loyal to Ralph?

2. What rationalization do Ralph and Piggy arrive at concerning their role in Simon's death?

3. What does Jack plan to do in order to enable his followers to have another feast?

4. Why is Roger so excited at the prospect of the beating of Willard?

5. What sacrifice to the beast does Jack order?

6. Why will it be so difficult for Ralph's group to keep the fire going?

7. How does Ralph suggest Piggy contact his aunt?

8. Who does Ralph fight during the attack?

9. What does Ralph's attacker do to him during the fight?

10. What did the attackers steal?

Answers

1. Piggy, Samneric, and some littluns remain with Ralph.

2. Ralph and Piggy rationalize that they were on the outside of the circle and did not really help beat Simon to death.

3. Jack plans to steal Piggy's glasses to start a fire.

4. Roger is excited because he will be able to indulge his own dark desires under Jack's irresponsible rule.

5. Jack orders his hunters to always sacrifice the head of their kills to the beast.

6. Ralph's group cannot keep the fire going because they are so few and Piggy will not help with the physical labor.

7. Ralph suggests Piggy should write a letter to his Aunt.

8. Ralph accidentally fights Eric during the attack.

9. Eric knees Ralph between the legs.

10. The attackers steal Piggy's glasses.

Suggested Essay Topics

1. How do Ralph, Piggy, and Samneric react to their roles in Simon's death? What does this tell you about them? What does it tell you about the boys in general? How is this experience related to Golding's theme that the flaws of mankind are inherent in man's nature?

2. Examine and compare the two groups' relationship to fire. What is significant about fire keepers versus fire takers or fire makers versus those who only want to use it to cook meat?

Chapter 11: "Castle Rock"

Summary

It is dawn on the beach, and Samneric watch as Ralph tries unsuccessfully to restart the fire from embers in the ashes. "Piggy sat expressionless behind the luminous wall of his myopia." He is livid over the loss of his glasses, insisting Ralph call a meeting, even though it is only him, Ralph, and Samneric.

Ralph blows the conch and Piggy takes it and says, "I can't see no more and I got to get my glasses back. Awful things has been done on this island. I voted for you for chief. He's the only one who ever got anything done. So now you speak, Ralph, and tell us what. Or else—."

Ralph tries to respond but is unable to bring his response to a definite point. He labors the point that they would have given the fire to Jack if he had asked, and now they cannot build a signal fire for rescue. He is unable to say more.

Piggy insists that Ralph do something. Ralph considers washing and brushing their hair and going civilly, to prove they aren't savages. Sam suggests taking spears and Piggy defiantly refuses. He declares he is going to tell Jack Merridew what he feels in a proper manner. The others tell him he will get hurt and he replies, "What can he do more than he has?" Piggy insists on carrying the conch when he goes, telling them:

> 'I'm going to him with this conch in my hands. I'm going to hold it out. Look, I'm goin' to say, you're stronger than I am and you haven't got asthma. You can see, I'm goin' to say, and with both eyes. But I don't ask for my glasses back, not as a favor. I don't ask you to be a sport, I'll say, not because you're strong, but because what's right's right. Give me my glasses, I'm going to say—you got to!'

Moved by Piggy's emotional appeal, Ralph agrees to try. He gives the conch to Piggy, who flushes with pride at carrying it. They eat some fruit, discuss their appearance, and Ralph again suggests cleaning up. Eventually they decide to go as they are. Ralph declares that Jack and his group will be no better.

Eric points out that Jack and his group are painted. "The others nodded. They understood only too well the liberation into savagery that the concealing paint brought." Eric again suggests painting themselves and Ralph yells "No paint!" He screams at them that they need smoke. Piggy adds, too hastily, that it's for rescue. "I knew that," shouted Ralph . . . "I knew it all the time. I hadn't forgotten." Piggy backs down. The twins stare at Ralph "as though they were seeing him for the first time."

They move toward Castle Rock, and stealthily approach behind the tall grass. They see smoke from the fire, a thin wisp. They step out of the grass. All but Piggy are armed with spears. They advance slowly. Roger, on sentry, stops them and demands identification. Ralph tells him, "You can see who I am . . . Stop being silly." He blows the conch loudly and Jack's followers appear, "painted out of recognition."

He announces he is calling an assembly. No one moves. Ralph starts forward and leaves Piggy kneeling on the stone bridge behind. Roger watches them carefully with his hand on the lever of the rock poised over the bridge.

Ralph declares an assembly. There is silence. He declares it again and demands to see Jack. The group makes excuses for Jack, but then Jack appears from the jungle, his features hidden by paint, but "identifiable by personality and red hair." His followers emerge from the jungle carrying the headless corpse of a pig.

Jack tells him to go, but Ralph angrily asks about Piggy's glasses, and Ralph calls Jack a thief. Jack rushes him with his spear. Ralph parries and lashes Jack across the face with his own spear. They spar again and stand facing each other, keeping just out of reach.

Piggy desperately tries to remind Ralph not to forget why they came. Ralph remembers, puts down his spear and appeals to Jack for Piggy's glasses. He looks into Jack's painted face and cannot remember what he used to look like. He reminds the others that they need the signal fire also. They will be here forever without it.

Jack's tribe laughs at him and Ralph is enraged. He calls them "painted fools" and explains how he is unable to keep the fire going with so few people helping. Jack orders them taken and his followers obey. "Samneric protested out of the heart of civilization," but their spears are taken and they are clumsily tied up.

Jack goads Ralph. "See? They do what I want." Ralph's temper breaks and he screams at Jack, "You're a beast and a swine and a bloody, bloody thief!" He charges Jack and they fight. Behind them, Piggy begs to speak. He holds up the conch and surprisingly, all quiet down. Roger, his one hand still on the lever, throws stones at Piggy but misses.

Piggy lifts the shell and says, "Which is better—to be a pack of painted Indians like you are, or to be sensible like Ralph is? . . . Which is better—to have rules and agree, or to hunt and kill? . . . Which is better, law and rescue, or hunting and breaking things up?"

As Piggy speaks, Jack backs up to his tribe and prepares to rush them. Above, Roger, "with a delirious sense of abandonment," releases his rock.

> The rock struck Piggy a glancing blow from chin to knee; the conch exploded into a thousand white fragments and ceased to exist. Piggy, saying nothing, with no time for even a grunt, traveled through the air sideways from the rock, turning over as he went. The rock bounded twice and was lost in the forest. Piggy fell forty feet on his back across that square red rock in the sea. His head opened and stuff came out and turned red. Piggy's arms and legs twitched a bit, like a pig's after it has been killed. Then the sea breathed again in a long, slow sigh, the water boiled white and pink over the rock; and when it went, sucking back again, the body of Piggy was gone.

Jack screams that that's what Ralph will get. The conch is gone. He is chief now. He hurls his spear at Ralph, grazing his side. The others, including Roger, hurl their spears as well. Ralph turns and flees, leaps over the headless body of the pig, and disappears into the forest.

Jack starts to pursue him, but stops at the pig and orders the others back to the fort. Roger has joined them to look at Piggy. The others avoid him slightly because of the new "hangman's horror [that] clung around him."

Jack begins brutally probing Samneric and asking them why they came to him with spears. Roger tells him, "That's not the way." Then, "Roger edged past the chief, only just avoiding pushing him

with his shoulder. The yelling ceased, and Samneric lay looking up in quiet terror. Roger advanced upon them as one wielding a nameless authority."

Analysis

For one last time, Ralph is in control, with Piggy as his secondary advisor. He remembers why they need smoke, and he manfully leads the expedition to Jack's in a last-ditch attempt to regain civilized ways on the island. His identity is intact, while Jack's and his followers have obscured themselves completely, and, having abandoned themselves totally to savagery, are completely hidden behind their paint.

The destruction of the conch and the death of blind Piggy are the climax of Golding's thesis. At this point, the boys have truly descended irreversibly into savagery due to the defects in their personalities. Jack has completely lost himself in his twisted vision, and he rules in an authoritarian manner behind an anonymous mask. Ralph's inability to understand the reasoning behind his desire for civilization and rules has made his leadership truly ineffective, with tragic results. Piggy's blind faith in a system of rules has failed him, and he never understood why. His vision gone, he is as dispensable as his namesakes, the island pigs. The boys have blindly allowed Jack to lead them down his path, and their identities are obscured behind the paint as well. They give Jack their unquestioning faith, as long as he gives them pleasure in return.

It is really only Roger who has received satisfaction from the entire situation. Unlike Jack, there is no sense of regret or wrongdoing in Roger. His sadistic tendencies are given full reign, and he comes into his own. He kills Piggy with "delirious abandonment." His rock-throwing episode, from earlier in the novel when he abused Henry, is repeated with a graver intensity. In the end, when he brushes past Jack, almost pushing him with his shoulder, it is easy to imagine who the next leader on the island will be, and in what direction Jack's brand of authority is heading. The destructive power released by Roger when he rolled the rock is indicative of the brute force that is only one step beyond Jack's authoritarian rule. Roger's chilling approach toward the twins ends the chapter, and hints what is to come in the book for the boys.

Of course, the destruction of the conch, and its truly blind devotee, marks the end of all vestiges of civilization on the island.

Study Questions

1. In the beginning of the chapter, what does Piggy tell Ralph to do with the conch?
2. What reason will Piggy give Jack for the return of his glasses?
3. What does Ralph declare their appearance will be when they approach Jack?
4. Who challenges the boys on their approach to Castle Rock?
5. When Jack appears, what has he been doing?
6. What does Ralph call Jack that provokes a fight?
7. What happens to Samneric after the fight?
8. What is Roger doing during Piggy's plea for a return to decency?
9. Who releases the rock that kills Piggy and destroys the conch?
10. Who takes over the questioning of Samneric from Jack at the chapter's end?

Answers

1. Piggy tells Ralph to blow the conch to call for an assembly.
2. Piggy will tell Jack to return them because it is the right thing to do.
3. Ralph declares they will wear "No paint!" when they approach Jack.
4. Roger challenges Ralph's approaching party.
5. Jack has been hunting. He has a headless pig corpse with him.
6. Ralph calls Jack a thief.
7. Samneric are disarmed and captured by Jack's tribe.
8. Roger throws rocks at Piggy.

9. Roger releases the rock.

10. Roger takes over the questioning of Samneric from Jack.

Suggested Essay Topics

1. Trace Roger's evolution from "dark boy" to sadist. What behavior has he expressed that has gradually led him to evolve into a frightening and dangerous figure? How is he a natural extension of Jack's authority? What place does the future hold for Roger on the island?

2. Examine Piggy's last day of life on the island. What does it say about his character and his role on the island? What does he do? Why does he do it? How does his death contribute to the symbolism of the boys' descent toward savagery?

Chapter 12: "Cry of the Hunters"

New Character:

Naval officer: *He is the first ashore from the rescue ship to encounter the boys.*

Summary

Ralph lay in hiding in the jungle assessing his wounds. He is close to Castle Rock for his pursuers did not follow him far. He glimpses a savage he believed was Bill, but "This was a savage whose image refused to blend with that ancient picture of a boy in shorts and shirt."

As the afternoon wanes, he sneaks closer and sees Robert, armed with a spear, idly manning a sentry post. Behind Robert, a cooking fire is roasting the pig. Ralph's mouth waters. A figure gives Robert a piece of meat and Robert begins to eat. Ralph retreats to eat some fruit, knowing he is momentarily safe as the feast progresses. He also knows that any bond between he and Jack is gone, and Jack will pursue him forever. "No," he rationalizes. "They're not as bad as that. It was an accident."

He approaches the fruit, and two littluns, frightened of his bloodied appearance, run off. He eats and approaches the empty shelters. He cannot stay there for he is too alone. He wishes to try again with Jack so he walks toward Castle Rock again.

He wanders into Simon's old hiding place and sees the pig's head mounted on a stick. It is only bone now, having been picked clean by the flies. He knows the skull is significant, but cannot understand why. It stares at him and grins.

> The skull regarded Ralph like one who knows all the answers but won't tell. A sick fear and rage swept him. Fiercely he hit out at the filthy thing in front of him that bobbed like a toy and came back, still grinning into his face, so that he lashed and cried out in loathing. Then he was licking his bruised knuckles and looking at the bare stick, while the skull lay in two pieces, its grin now six feet across. He wrenched

the quivering stick from the crack and held it as a spear between him and the white pieces. Then he backed away, keeping his face to the skull that lay grinning at the sky.

That night, Ralph stealthily approaches Castle Rock, where he sees another armed sentry. He feels his own isolation acutely. He moans as he rests and finds he cannot sleep despite his weariness. He longs to walk among his friends and have all the old ways back. But instead, he lies alone, knowing he is an outcast, "Cos I had some sense." He listens to the familiar chant from Castle Rock, "*Kill the beast! Cut his throat! Spill his blood!*"

Presently, two sentries replace the single guard and Ralph sadly recognizes their shape. Samneric are now part of Jack's tribe. After a bit, he approaches them and calls out to them. They do not hear him and he must call out louder. He is worried because the only weapon he has is the spear that held up the pig's skull.

He safely gets their attention and they tell him he must leave. Ralph tells them he came to see them. He notices they are painted and that they are ashamed of this. Samneric tells him again to leave. They tell Ralph they were made to join the tribe, and that Jack and Roger hate him and plan to hunt him in the morning. They tell Ralph that they will form a line across the island and hunt him like a pig. Ralph asks what they will do when they catch him. Samneric give him some meat and tell him that Roger has sharpened a stick at both ends. It is clear from their reply that they fear Roger more than Jack, that he did something awful to them to force them to join the tribe. Ralph leaves. He cannot comprehend the significance of the sharpened stick. Behind him, he hears Samneric arguing with someone. He eats the meat and settles into some vines for a deep sleep.

He awakes next morning to the sound of the hunters pursuing him. Ralph hides in an indentation left by the rock that killed Piggy. He hears Jack, Roger, and one of the twins approaching. Roger is torturing the twin to reveal where he had spoken to Ralph the night before. The twin, in pain, reveals the position. They begin to roll rocks off Castle Rock and into the thicket to flush him out. They roll a huge rock down and almost crush him. Then two savages surround his thicket and thrust spears in. Ralph thrusts back and wounds someone. They cannot reach him in the thicket.

Presently he smells smoke and realizes they are trying to burn him out. Ralph flees and attacks a small savage blocking his path. He gets past and they pursue him, tightening the cordon around him, not giving him time to think.

He considers breaking the line, climbing a tree, or hoping they will pass. None of these are attractive alternatives for him. He decides to hide and retreats into what used to be Simon's secret place. The fire approaches, leaving a huge curtain of smoke between the island and the sun. He hears the fire as it prepares to consume the fruit trees, and he wonders what they will eat tomorrow.

A savage approaches him, but doesn't see him. A herd of pigs, flushed by the fire and the hunters, runs by. Ralph prepares to attack. The fear of the implied purpose of the sharpened stick drives him. The savage sticks his face in the thicket. Ralph charges him and gets past. A spear flies past him as he runs. He avoids a bush that bursts into flames. He passes the shelters as they burst into flames. He falls onto the beach and rolls over and over with his arm up, preparing to beg for mercy.

Ralph looks up into the face of a uniformed naval officer peering at him curiously. He asks Ralph if there are any adults around. Dazed, Ralph shakes his head. The savages emerge from the jungle and look at the naval officer.

"Fun and games," the officer guesses. Then behind the boys, the jungle bursts into flames. "We saw your smoke. What have you been doing? Having a war or something?"

Ralph tells him two have been killed. The officer is astonished, both at the deaths and at the appalling appearance of the children. Others emerge from the jungle. Percival Wemys Madison approaches the officer and attempts to recite the litany of his name, address, and phone number, but this time he cannot even remember his name.

The officer tells Ralph they will rescue them and asks how many there are. Ralph does not know. The officer asks who's boss and Ralph tells him he is. Jack, standing in the background, unpainted now and wearing the remains of his choir cap, starts forward at this, then stops. Piggy's glasses still hang on his belt.

The officer is appalled at the lack of organization. "I should have thought that a pack of British boys—you're all British, aren't you?—would have been able to put up a better show than that. . . . " Ralph tries to explain that they cooperated at first.

"The officer nodded helpfully. 'I know. Jolly good show. Like *The Coral Island.*'" Ralph just stares at him. Then he thinks of the lost beauty of the island, Simon and Piggy, and he begins to weep. Others join him. "Ralph wept for the end of innocence, the darkness of man's heart, and the fall through the air of the true, wise friend called Piggy."

The officer is embarrassed by this display. "He turned away to give them time to pull themselves together; and waited, allowing his eyes to rest on the trim cruiser in the distance."

Analysis

It is obvious that Roger has tortured Samneric into submission and has dark plans for Ralph. This is never quite revealed, but the sharpened stick suggests Roger's previous anal impalement of the wounded pig, and the mounting of the first sacrifice to the beast.

Ralph's contemplation of the skull of the Lord of the Flies is significant. He does not understand it, as he has not understood the lack of cooperation on the island previously. All of Ralph's inability to comprehend stem from his not recognizing the beast inherent in his own nature. He does not understand Jack's desire to hunt, he does not understand why he must maintain order, and he does not remember why they need the fire for good things. Even as he confronts the face of the beast, he is not a deep enough thinker to understand. Like all violence, the end result of destruction is that it consumes itself like a disease in a dying body. The flies have consumed the flesh of the pig, and only the skull is left. Still, Ralph's attempt to destroy it only results in the skull breaking and appearing larger than before. Then, without knowing why, his instincts for self-preservation take over and he takes the spear. He is willing to fight and kill to survive. He is willing to use the beast to survive. He does not see the connection that his actions have caused the beast to become larger and more powerful just as his striking out at the skull caused it to split into a larger grin.

The bitter irony of the story's end is that the smoke the boys use to flush Ralph for the kill is the signal for their rescue. Jack, or perhaps even Roger, unleash their power in order to kill Ralph: the last remaining vestige of civilization. They do not seem to care, or perhaps they do not understand, that what they have done will destroy them all. Like Ralph, Jack is unable to see the other side of his own nature. Ironically, it is Ralph's vision that is realized when a ship arrives after having spotted their smoke.

The officer, representing newly discovered civilization, is appalled at the condition of the children. He cannot understand why they were not able to carry on like good British schoolboys and behave like the children in *The Coral Island*. But, like Ralph and Jack, he does not see the duality of his own nature. He is on the beach, shocked at the boys' lack of civilization, yet he is an officer on a boat in which the main function is to hunt and kill.

The boys' true loss of innocence is expressed when Percival Wemys Madison, whose only flimsy hold on the past was his memorized name, phone number, and address, can no longer even remember his name.

Ralph is unable again to express the truth behind his actions. He accepts responsibility for the island and weeps for the loss of innocence. Like Simon, he has come to a true understanding of the Lord of the Flies, or the "darkness of man's heart." For the first time he seems to recognize the true value of Piggy.

Jack stands cowardly in the background. He has removed his makeup and put on his choir hat. Only Piggy's glasses on his belt remain as a testament to his savagery. He wisely declines to accept leadership responsibility now that blame will probably be assigned. Like a true anarchist, he is able to shed his personality if it will suit his purpose.

Golding's final irony lies in the person of the naval officer. He is appalled at the savagery of the children. He is embarrassed by their behavior and lack of decorum, and he is amazed at how easily they reverted to warlike ways. Yet when he looks away from their savagery, his gaze settles on the craft he arrived and will leave in, a battle cruiser, an efficient weapon of war. Like Ralph and Jack, and the dirty children in front of him, he cannot comprehend the violent tendencies of his own nature. Like Ralph, he clings to a code of civilization he does not understand. Like Jack, he unquestioningly follows his primitive desires.

The beautiful island burns behind them. It is a metaphor for society and the world, a paradise, destroyed by the primitive instincts of man. Golding has proven his point within the restrictive confines of his story. The children of the island all possessed flaws that lead to their inevitable moral destruction, as represented by the physical destruction of the island. The fire that would have consumed them all, like the fire of the all-consuming war, is the power of the beast released. In each case, the characters contributed to the eventual destruction of their island, as the war and the rest of mankind is destroying the world.

Ralph clung to a belief in order, without ever recognizing his own savage instincts. He occasionally succumbed to them, but never understood them. This was why he was able to fail as a leader and an organizer.

Piggy held stubbornly to a belief in order and intellectual thought, but his inability to understand chaos, or even allow for it a little, caused his death. His blind insistence on order tended to bring out the worst in Jack and Roger, and his isolation by pomposity and physical laziness did not make his viewpoint any more appealing to the others.

Jack was the antithesis of Ralph, yet mirrored Ralph's inability to see the other side of his nature. He was violent and anarchic, and sought rule by absolute power. His belief in his own authoritarian rules would have eventually lead to the destruction of them all.

Roger was, like Jack, a product of anarchy on the island. His own perverse character was emerging unfettered as civilization on the island gradually disappeared. He was probably the next in line for leadership, as his brute force was the direction Jack's administration was heading. His contempt for Jack was even beginning to show when he took over the task of torturing Samneric, and he one-upped Jack's regime of fear by killing Piggy. He is the worst in terms of what Golding says lay hidden in man's nature.

Finally, Simon, able to see the beast, yet unable to tell the others the truth, becomes the truest victim of the beast. His death is the death of truth and beauty, powerful enough to spot the beast, but too fragile to fight the inherent flaws of humanity.

In the end, the cyclical nature of events in the novel returns the boys to the war-torn world from which they came, removing them from the war-torn world in which they created and lived.

On a final note, the two major characters without violent tendencies, Piggy and Simon, do not survive. They are unable to recognize their own id (as mentioned in the beginning of the guide as the modern equivalent of Beelzebub in man's nature), which ensures the survival of the host at all costs, and therefore lack the inherent ability to survive. The death of wisdom (Piggy) and spirituality (Simon) become inevitable on the island as the other boys progress toward savagery. This parallels the events in the outside world of Golding's novel (as the atomic war rages on), and perhaps in the real world that Golding witnessed during World War II. The message contained therein, then, must be that spiritually and intellectually, mankind cannot survive as the modern world careens towards chaos and destruction.

Study Questions

1. Where does Ralph first hide from his pursuers?

2. Who gives Ralph meat from Jack's feast?

3. Why did Samneric join Jack's tribe?

4. What has Roger prepared for Ralph?

5. How does Jack's tribe flush Ralph from hiding?

6. What does Ralph discover when he flees to the beach?

7. How does Jack appear on the beach?

8. What boy cannot remember his name?

9. Who takes responsibility for the events on the island?

10. Why is the naval officer disappointed in the boys?

Answers

1. Ralph hides in the bushes near Castle Rock.

2. Sam gives Ralph some meat.

3. Samneric were tortured by Roger until they joined the tribe.

4. Roger has prepared a stick sharpened at both ends for Ralph.

5. Jack's tribe flushes Ralph by setting the jungle on fire.

6. Ralph discovers a ship has come to rescue them.

7. When Jack appears on the beach, he has put on his choir cap. Piggy's glasses are on his belt, but he is not described as wearing his makeup.

8. Percival Wemys Madison cannot remember his name.

9. Ralph takes responsibility by admitting to being the leader. Jack considers speaking up, but is silent.

10. The naval officer is disappointed because the boys did not behave like the good little British schoolchildren in *Coral Island.*

Suggested Essay Topics

1. Choose any of the main characters whose personalities are described in detail (Ralph, Jack, Simon, Piggy, Roger) and trace their development in the story as it pertains to Golding's theory that the basic flaw of mankind is inherent in man. Support your thesis with character details highlighting their flaws or descent into savagery.

2. Throughout the story, trace the symbolic role of fire. Begin with the raging fire that kills the small boy, consider the changing role of fire between Jack's tribe and Ralph's, and finish with the fire that destroys the island and brings rescue.

Sample Analytical Paper Topics

The following paper topics are designed to test your under-standing of the novel as a whole and your ability to analyze important themes and literary devices. Following each question is a sample outline to help get you started.

Topic #1

The characters' loss of identity is a predominant theme of the book. Discuss each of the main characters' loss of identity as the book progresses, and how this brings about the devastation that occurs in the book.

Outline

I.   Thesis statement: *The main characters in* Lord of the Flies *experience a loss of identity throughout the book that eventually causes the devastation and death that prevail.*

II. Ralph

    A. His original view of the island as a paradise

    B. His leadership qualities and ideas

    C. Ineffective leadership

    D. Inability to remember his purpose

    E. His own minor digressions into savagery

III. Piggy

    A. Piggy's introduction and the significance of his naming

    B. The rejection and acceptance of his ideas

    C. Piggy's changing relationship with Ralph

    D. Piggy's symbolic descent into blindness

IV. Jack Merridew

    A. Jack's original role on the island

    B. Jack's leadership qualities

    C. The gradual symbolic camouflage

    D. Jack's twisted vision

V. Roger

    A. Roger's initial description

    B. Roger's bizarre behavioral tendencies unfettered by civilized restraint

    C. Roger's emerging role in Jack's tribe

VI. *Conclusion:* Why the characters' loss of their civilized identities support Golding's theory that the problems with mankind are inherent in man.

Topic #2

Beelzebub, the demon of chaos, is also known as the Lord of the Flies. Though this is not referred to directly in the book, chaos, violence, anarchy, and destruction are central images in the book. Trace the characters' relationships to the Lord of the Flies in the book, particularly as it is physically represented by the pig's head impaled on a stick.

Outline

I. Thesis statement: *Each of the main characters in* Lord of the Flies *has a significant relationship with "the beast" on the island that is connected with the emerging scenes of violence on the island and their fates.*

II. Ralph

    A. Leader and champion of civilization

    B. Opposite of Jack

    C. Minor forays into violence, anarchy, or chaos

        1. Standing the boar's charge and participating in the dance

        2. Fighting with Jack

        3. Forgetting his purpose

    D. Major forays into violence, anarchy, or chaos

        1. His role in Simon's death

        2. Battling his attackers

    E. Ralph's inability to destroy the Lord of the Flies

        1. His encounter with the skull

        2. Loss of control on the island

III. Jack

    A. His increasing desire to hunt

    B. His decreasing desire for responsibility

    C. His increasing desire for power

    D. Denunciation of the conch

    E. Harbinger of anarchy

        1. His own tribe on Castle Rock

        2. His own brand of leadership

        3. The hunt for Ralph

IV. Piggy

    A. Intellect vs. manual labor

    B. Frail belief in the conch

    C. Inability to accept chaos

    D. Victim of violence

V. Simon

    A. Understanding the nature of the beast

    B. Discussions with the pig's head

        1. Talking from within himself

        2. Falling into the pig's mouth

    C. The inability to express the truth

    D. Looking into the face of the beast

    E. Victim of violence

VI. Roger

    A. The emerging sadist

    B. Behavioral abnormalities

        1. Descriptions of his eager embracing of the collapse of authority

    C. Champion of anarchy

VII. *Conclusion*: Sum up the boys' relationships with "the beast" in terms of their fates.

Topic #3

A subtle thematic device in the book is Golding's use of point of view to establish character and motives. Trace the book's shifting point of view in these terms.

Outline

I. Thesis statement: *Though Ralph is the main character of* Lord of the Flies, *and much of the story is told from his point of view, Golding also reveals his narrative through other characters, most notably Jack and Simon, as well as an omnipresent narrator. These separate views help to establish both character and theme.*

II.   Ralph

    A.   The novel's predominant point of view

    B.   Plain, descriptive prose

    C.   Prose lapses into poetical visions

III. Jack

    A.   The hunter's perspective

    B.   Motivations for anarchy

    C.   What kind of language?

IV.   Simon

    A.   The poetical view of the island

    B.   Character through vision

    C.   Introspection

V.   Ralph, Jack, Simon

    A.   The significance of the candle-buds

VI.   Omnipresent narrator

    A.   Instances of

    B.   Purpose of

    C.   Prose style of

VII. *Conclusion*: Even more than a narrative device, Golding's shifting narration serves an integral function in the novel.

SECTION FOUR

Bibliography

Quotations from *Lord of the Flies* were taken from the following translation:

Golding, William. *Lord of the Flies*. New York: Capricorn Books, G.P. Putnam's Sons, 1954.

Some biographical information, Golding's interpretation of his own theme, the brief discussion of Beelzebub as the "Lord of the Flies" that appear in the author biography, and information contained in the Introduction were taken from E.L. Epstein's biographical and critical notes that follow the above edition of the novel.

The following sources were also consulted for the preparation of this manuscript:

The New Grolier Multimedia Encyclopedia on CD ROM. Online Computer Systems, Inc. The Software Toolworks, Inc. Reproduced for Apple, 1993.

TIME Almanac Reference Edition on CD ROM. Washington, D.C.: Compact Publishing, Inc., and *TIME* Inc. Magazine Co., 1994.

Riley, Carolyn, ed. *Contemporary Literary Criticism*: CLC 1. Detroit: Gale Research Co., 1973.

Ryan, Bryan, ed. *Major 20th Century Writers*. Detroit: Gale Research Inc., 1991. 2:E-K, 1206.

Introducing...

MAXnotes

REA's Literature Study Guides

MAXnotes™ offer a fresh look at masterpieces of literature, presented in a liv
and interesting fashion. **MAXnotes**™ offer the essentials of what you should kn
about the work, including outlines, explanations and discussions of the pl
character lists, analyses, and historical context. **MAXnotes**™ are designed to h
you think independently about literary works by raising various issues and thoug
provoking ideas and questions. Written by literary experts who currently teach t
subject, **MAXnotes**™ enhance your understanding and enjoyment of the work.

Available **MAXnotes**™ include the following:

Animal Farm	**The Great Gatsby**	**Moby-Dick**
Beowulf	**Hamlet**	**1984**
Brave New World	**Huckleberry Finn**	**Of Mice and Men**
The Canterbury Tales	**I Know Why the**	**The Odyssey**
The Catcher in the Rye	**Caged Bird Sings**	**Paradise Lost**
The Crucible	**The Iliad**	**Plato's Republic**
Death of a Salesman	**Julius Caesar**	**A Raisin in the Sun**
Divine Comedy I-Inferno	**King Lear**	**Romeo and Juliet**
Gone with the Wind	**Les Misérables**	**The Scarlet Letter**
The Grapes of Wrath	**Lord of the Flies**	**A Tale of Two Cities**
Great Expectations	**Macbeth**	**To Kill a Mockingbird**

RESEARCH & EDUCATION ASSOCIATION
61 Ethel Road W. • Piscataway, New Jersey 08854
Phone: (908) 819-8880

Please send me more information about MAXnotes™.

Name _____

Address _____

City _____ State _____ Zip _____